CAKELOVE

IN THE MORNING

CAKELOVE

IN THE MORNING

RECIPES FOR
Muffins, Scones, Pancakes, Waffles,
Biscuits, Frittatas,
and Other Breakfast Treats

WARREN BROWN

Photographs by Joshua Cogan

STEWART, TABORI & CHANG | NEW YORK

Published in 2012 by Stewart, Tabori & Chang
An imprint of ABRAMS

Copyright © 2012 Warren Brown
Photographs copyright © 2012 Joshua Cogan

Library of Congress Cataloging-in-Publication Data

Brown, Warren, 1970-
Cakelove in the morning / Warren Brown.
p. cm.
Includes index.
ISBN 978-1-58479-894-1
1. Bread. 2. Breakfasts. 3. Baked products. 4. Cooking (Eggs). 5.
Cookbooks. I. CakeLove (Bakery) II. Title.
TX769.B838 2012
641.81'5—dc23
2011032784

Editor: Jennifer Levesque
Designer: Alissa Faden
Production Manager: Jules Thomson

The text of this book was composed in Lubalin Graph, Gotham, and Neutraface.

Printed and bound in China

10 9 8 7 6 5 4 3 2 1

Stewart, Tabori & Chang books are available at special discounts when purchased in quantity for premiums and promotions as well as fundraising or educational use. Special editions can also be created to specification. For details, contact specialsales@abramsbooks.com or the address below.

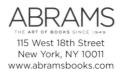

ABRAMS
THE ART OF BOOKS SINCE 1949
115 West 18th Street
New York, NY 10011
www.abramsbooks.com

CONTENTS

INTRODUCTION

I began cooking all the way back in grade school.
My mother rightfully thought my sisters and
I should know our way around the kitchen, so we
traded off on lunch duty. The first full meal
I ever cooked was a Sunday brunch. I knew then
and there that my future would somehow be
centered around the kitchen.

BY HIGH SCHOOL, omelets had become the center of my world. I made them huge—as large as possible, filled with everything I could chop, dice, and sauté, laying it all on a bed of fluffy eggs under a blanket of cheese. I especially liked it when the spatula bent under the weight of each family-size monster. I'm glad to say that my interests have broadened.

My inspiration for the recipes in this book comes from years of happy times and family gatherings around the breakfast or brunch table, especially for holidays and special occasions. Whether it was my dad and his pancake breakfasts, French toast prepared by my mom, brunch at Stouffers Hotel in Terminal Tower, right in the heart of downtown Cleveland, or Mother's Day breakfast-in-bed served to my mother by my sisters and me, breakfast has been the basis for many memories that I treasured long after the meal was over.

I really love the whole experience of brunch: the gathering of friends and family in a relaxed atmosphere, everyone grazing for hours on all types of food. Conquering the enormity of any brunch buffet has been a real challenge over the years; I've even developed the habit of munching on a few pieces of fresh cantaloupe when I feel full—somehow that settles everything in my stomach to make room for more!

I hope this book dispels the myth that you have to wake up at the crack of dawn to cook a good breakfast from scratch. There are a number of recipes included here that can be prepared very quickly—or made in advance to have on hand and grab quickly while on the run.

But if you don't have to rush, then don't—especially when it comes to brunch. It's usually the only meal of the day anyway, so a few extra minutes spent cooking this or baking that won't hurt. Brunch is for the weekends when, hopefully, we're all taking time out from the rest of our life. And that's why I love it. The food is great, but it's all about the time I can take to kick back and leisurely prepare something fun that I can eat while enjoying the company of my family. There's simply nothing else I'd rather be doing.

Another thing I love about the recipes in this book is that so many cross over with baking cakes. One way or another, the core ingredients—butter, sugar, grains, eggs—make an appearance on just about every page. This helps keep the shopping list short! But the real bonus is that the more comfortable you are with baking, the easier it will be to follow the directions for each recipe. And if you're not an experienced baker, don't fret: I like to break down every recipe so you're guided every step of the way.

And yes, while a balanced breakfast is an important part of a healthy diet, these pages are filled with rich foods that make it easy to want seconds. Go ahead, because if you're really enjoying brunch, you can put the diet on hold. This isn't cooking for every day, so we can make room for a treat.

Creating and cooking my way through these recipes allowed me to keep a safe distance from the type of baking we do every day at CakeLove. It brought me back to those early years in my parents' kitchen when the world was my omelet—and I fell in love with cooking all over again.

Happy baking!

MAIN INGREDIENTS

Always use the best ingredients available. Make sure your eggs are fresh and your spices even more so. Choose quality bacon and sausage, not the kinds filled with nitrates and other chemicals. Cook with the seasons when it comes to fruits and vegetables. These recipes are very adaptable, so I encourage you to make substitutions—especially when it's a question of quality.

FLOUR Unless otherwise noted, my flour of choice is General Mills brand unbleached all-purpose flour. Ninety-nine percent of the time I measure by weight. A scale is your best bet for success. But if a recipe calls for less than four tablespoons of flour, go ahead and skip the scale. I always sift the flour directly into a bowl set on a scale. Five ounces equals one cup. It's really important to be precise with measurements when baking—especially with cakes—and flour is the most important item to measure correctly.

PASTRY FLOUR is a low-protein flour that leads to a very tender baked good. If you don't have pastry flour, substitute a mix of 9 parts of all-purpose or whole-wheat flour to 1 part potato starch.

POTATO STARCH is gluten-free and lightens up the texture of baked goods while delivering just a hint of flavor. Potato starch is readily available in major grocery stores: Check the specialty baking or wheat-free product aisle; you may also find it in the kosher foods section. If all else fails, purchase a two-pound bag online. It will last a long time.

SUGAR Superfine granulated sugar is the default sugar for all of the recipes. The grains are a little bit smaller than the standard "granulated" sugar and yield a finer texture when used in baked goods. It's a little less than eight ounces per cup if you're using a very sensitive scale, but rounding up will do. If you need to use regular granulated sugar, just give it a few pulses in the food processor to break it down a bit.

TURBINADO SUGAR is an unrefined, large-crystal sugar, almost as coarse as kosher salt. It's fantastic as an exterior coating—use it to create a crunchy effect.

MILK A lot of the recipes call for milk, which, naturally, means cow's milk. At home I find myself doing a lot of baking with either a lactose-free cow's milk or unsweetened soy milk. Vanilla-flavored soy milk works just as well and is a little easier going down the hatch if you're trying it for the first time. Soy milk can be substituted in many of the recipes that call for milk, cream, or half-and-half, but the flavor and texture won't be quite as rich. If you're making this substitution, I recommend you try it first before serving it to a guest.

BUTTER I use the standard American unsalted butter available at every grocery store. Don't feel like you have to swap in an expensive or wildly exotic butter to achieve great results. Do you like the way your butter tastes on toast? If you do, you're in business.

COOKING OILS Using the highest quality oils for pan frying and sautéing will yield the best results, both in terms of taste and preventing your foods from burning. My preference is a high-quality rice bran oil, which happens to be the healthiest option, or grapeseed. Both withstand extremely high temperatures, have minimal absorption into the foods, and impart little taste. Canola oil will work perfectly well, too, and is much more economical and practical, especially for deep frying.

EGGS All eggs used are graded large. White or brown doesn't matter—the taste will be the same.

ON LACTOSE

If you're like me, lactose is not your friend, and many typical breakfast and brunch foods are off limits. Lactose intolerance is an unfortunate but very common affliction.

I have learned to live without cow's milk and, as a beverage, I don't miss it at all. I'm able to tolerate butter and cheese from goats or sheep without difficulty. For what it's worth, I can't see how we could ever handle cow's milk. We're nowhere near the size of a calf and couldn't possibly need all of the nutrients that come from a lactating cow. When cow's milk is cultured and given time to break down—as in cheese or yogurt—the lactose is broken down as well and made much more friendly to the human digestive system.

I eat active-culture yogurt on a regular basis, which helps me digest just about anything that's dairy—whether it's butter, cheese, or cream—no matter which animal is the source. If you haven't included active-culture yogurts into your diet but are lactose intolerant, look into it. Stay away from the artificially sweetened or heavily sweetened brands that dominate the supermarket aisles. Look for options that have low amounts of natural sweeteners to round out your diet.

FRUITS AND VEGETABLES Choose the freshest, all-natural fruits and vegetables available. The best way to make this happen is to shop at the local farmers markets or become involved in CSA—community supported agriculture. Freshly harvested produce that comes from a local farm supports your community and provides you and your family with better quality foods. The shorter transit time from field to market means that the produce has more time to grow and, hopefully, ripen on the vine as opposed to being picked well before its time and maturing by exposure to chemicals and gas sprays. Small, local farmers are much more likely to grow using organic methods or with minimal synthetic fertilizers. Their tradition of rotating crops that thrive under local growing conditions brings a well-balanced bounty of food that keeps the menu fresh and inviting.

To ripen fruit, it's always helpful to keep at least two in an enclosed space. I place fresh fruit under a cake dome. This way, fruit flies don't become a problem, the fruit has plenty of air to breathe, and gases that facilitate ripening can exchange between them. Placing fruit in a brown paper bag works just as well.

Thoroughly rinse your fruits and vegetables to reduce consumption of dirt, debris, microbial pathogens, and chemicals used during cultivation. Probably the best method to wash foods is to use a 3 parts water to 1 part white distilled vinegar solution. If there are lots of nooks and crannies, just soak them for a few minutes in the water-vinegar solution, then rinse with cold water. There are a lot of potential hazards to watch out for, so wash your hands and your fruits and vegetables well.

CUTTING BACK ON THE FAT

If you're feeling self-conscious about the amount of fat from butter and oils in your diet, you can easily cut back without sacrificing results with a few easy steps.

- For sautéing with butter, rub a cold stick of butter against the hot pan surface instead of slicing off tablespoons at a time.

- For oils, decant some into a spray bottle and use a few squeezes from the mist setting for a very thin, but sufficient, coating on the pan's surface. It can take several squeezes just to equal one teaspoon.

- Slightly reduce the temperature under the pan; the chances of food sticking will be reduced.

- Use very small amounts of oil to get the cooking started, then add in water as the item cooks to prevent sticking.

HERBS AND SPICES FOR THE MORNING

In the morning our palates are accustomed to relatively simple flavors. Although there's always room for a touch of flavor from the herb garden to give a dish a distinctive edge, in general I try to keep recipes straightforward and rooted in the simple flavors I'm preparing. I prefer using fresh herbs whenever possible, but don't let dried herbs stand in the way of your plans.

Still, breakfast wouldn't be the same without sweet-smelling brown spices such as cinnamon, nutmeg, allspice, and star anise. Always buy your spices in small amounts because they lose their flavor very quickly. Buy whole spices—especially nutmeg—and grind them yourself when you need them.

Good salt is important, too. I really respect the tremendous impact salt can have on a dish. Relative to other ingredients, it hardly tips the scales, but we can instantly recognize when there's too much or too little. That's impressive. I love the sharp texture of kosher salt, the softness of fleur de sel, the way just enough salt will warm the palate and wet the mouth.

And vanilla, the most glorious spice, is used in just about every baked good and anything that touches the griddle. Pure vanilla extract has no substitute. Don't fall for imitation or artificial vanillas—they don't deserve your attention. I always use Nielsen Massey Madagascar Bourbon vanilla extract, which is readily available at fine grocers. And keep in mind that wherever a vanilla bean is called for you can easily substitute 1 to 3 teaspoons of extract instead. Vanilla beans are hard to find, expensive, and very often extremely brittle—especially if sold individually in a jar. The best bet is to find a source that sells vanilla beans by the quarter pound and keep them wrapped together in a plastic bag.

EQUIPMENT

There's really no need to stock your kitchen with lots of fancy, expensive equipment—unless you want to!

HANDS There are no better tools than your hands, so they'll see a lot of action. Keep your nails short, massage your wrists and forearms, gently shake your hands and fingers when they tire, and wash them thoroughly before and after you cook.

KNIVES AND CUTTING BOARDS At least one sharp knife is essential. For someone who has excellent knife skills, a great chef's knife is like a handheld food processor. Even if you have a real food processor to speed up your prep, a good-quality knife will still be essential to get the vegetables and meats ready for the processor. A set of knives is great, but not as necessary as one great chef's knife.

Keep at least two cutting boards for your kitchen to reduce the chances of cross-contamination. With all of the concerns over foodborne illness, it's a good idea to take preventive measures at home and cut meats on one board and vegetables and fruits on another board. And, for the sake of taste, be sure to cut aromatic items like garlic, onions, and shallots on their own board.

MIXING BOWLS Keep plenty around because they're always handy. A lot of the recipes call for prepping and setting items aside, then tossing them all together. That requires space and the best thing to have is a bowl that's about two times larger than the items you want to mix. Otherwise, they seem to get legs and jump out of the bowl.

KITCHEN SHEARS, or any type of heavy-duty, dishwasher-safe scissors make quick work out of a lot of cutting tasks. I especially like them when cutting pieces of raw bacon into smaller strips or just to portion packaged bacon into a reasonable size.

SCOOPS AND LADLES of specific measure are helpful for controlling batters and making pancakes and waffles of consistent size. I use an ice cream scoop that holds ¼ cup of batter.

HEAVY-DUTY CASSEROLE DISHES with relatively high sides are very useful. I especially like the enamel-coated ones for their ability to insulate fragile ingredients like eggs from scorching.

HEAVY-DUTY FRYING PANS AND SAUCE POTS are a must for reliable cooking. High-quality pans can double-up as griddles for pancakes or French toast, too. I rarely use pans with a nonstick surface. Adequate amounts of butter or vegetable oil and careful attention to the cooking temperature are all we need to protect the food from sticking.

A STAND MIXER is very handy, for buttercreams as well as mixing batter for scones and cakes.

CAKE PANS Keep life simple and use old-fashioned aluminum cake pans. Always keep nonstick spray that includes starch in the pantry and use it liberally. I avoid nonstick pans because they create a very tough exterior on the cake. The batter needs to cling to the pan surface a little bit; otherwise, the sugars will bond together and make an edge that's unpleasant to bite through.

GRIDDLES AND WAFFLE IRONS Just be sure to get one that gets very hot. A lot of the modern ones just don't get to the temperature you need. Look online at resale websites or in secondhand stores for older units.

SPATULAS There are many different types of spatula, and just about every kind has a role in preparing the recipes in this book. I keep lots of flexible, siliconelike spatulas on hand because they're great for turning and folding gentle pancake, muffin, and waffle batters. Full-size metal spatulas are essential for flipping eggs—I use one with a broad head and beveled edge. I also cook my eggs in aluminum pans so I don't worry about scratching the surface of the pan. Offset metal spatulas are a must for cake decorating and can come in handy as egg turners.

FRENCH TOAST, PANCAKES, AND WAFFLES

When batter—or battered bread—meets a hot griddle, magic happens. French toast, pancakes, and waffles just scream "Sunday breakfast" to me, but, in truth, you can whip up most of these recipes anytime you want to make your family smile.

FRENCH TOAST

When I was growing up, French toast was one of the special treats in our house. Leave it to the French to come up with such a delicious way to use up day-old bread (they call it *pain perdu*, or "lost bread"). Plain old white bread will do in a pinch, but go for the egg-based challah or brioche and you'll see what a dream this breakfast was always meant to be.

French toast is so full of flavor that it really needs nothing more than a dusting of confectioners' sugar for serving. But don't let that stop you from adding maple syrup, fresh fruit, or whipped cream!

DON'T OVERSOAK the bread or it will disintegrate before you can get it into the pan.

START WITH good-quality unsliced bread, then cut the loaf into 1- to 2-inch slices depending on your preference.

YOU CAN USE white or multigrain bread, but a brioche loaf or challah will be more luxurious.

IT'S BETTER to work with bread that's two or three days old. A slice that's too delicate will fall apart once battered.

DEPENDING ON how hungry everyone is, one to two pieces of French toast (unstuffed) is a serving.

MY FAVORITE FRENCH TOAST

Just rich enough, and fragrantly laced with cinnamon, this is my idea of perfect French toast. This may seem like a lot of liquid, but the challah can soak up a lot, which means a lot more flavor, too.

Brioche or challah	1 loaf
Milk	3 to 4 cups
Eggs	6
Ground cinnamon	1 tablespoon
Vanilla extract	2 teaspoons
Unsalted butter or vegetable oil	1 tablespoon

1. Place a large skillet on the stove over medium heat and preheat the oven to 275°F to keep the finished French toast warm.

2. Cut the bread into 2-inch-thick slices. If you are making Stuffed French Toast (see page 21) use slices 2 inches thick and make a slit that goes halfway into the slice to create a pocket.

3. In a wide bowl or baking pan, whisk together the milk, eggs, cinnamon, and vanilla.

4. Soak each slice in the milk mixture for about 1 minute; 30 seconds per side. Don't oversaturate the bread or it will disintegrate in the pan.

5. Place the butter in the pan and let it coat the bottom to prevent the bread from sticking. Using 1 or 2 slices at a time, place the soaked bread in the pan and cook on one side for about 2 minutes.

6. Flip the toast using a metal spatula and cook on the opposite side. If you are making Stuffed French Toast, lift the top half of the pocket with a spatula, and spoon the stuffing into the pocket. Lightly pat down the top half of the bread over the stuffing.

7. Move the toast from the skillet to a heat-resistant plate in the preheated oven. Serve dusted with sugar or with maple syrup.

STUFFED FRENCH TOAST

Serve any of these variations and it's a sign that you're truly committed to creating magic. Slice the bread thick enough to provide a decent-size pocket. Each makes enough to generously fill 4 to 6 pieces of My Favorite French Toast.

Prepare My Favorite French Toast as directed on page 19. After flipping it over, spoon some of one of the following stuffings into the pocket. To serve, carefully lift the Stuffed French Toast with a large spatula and slide it onto each plate.

CREAM CHEESE STUFFING

This filling will ooze out of the bread and spread across the plate in a deliciously messy way.

Cream cheese **4 ounces (½ cup)**
Unsalted butter, softened **2 tablespoons**
Granulated sugar **4 ounces (½ cup)**
Confectioners' sugar **3 tablespoons**
Milk **2 tablespoons**

1. In the bowl of a stand mixer, combine the cream cheese and butter and beat on high speed for 30 seconds, then add the sugars and continue to beat until smooth and fluffy.

2. Reduce the speed to low and add in half of the milk. Beat on high speed until smooth. Add more milk as needed until the filling drizzles off a spoon.

APPLE CURLS

The combination of flavors is reminiscent of baked apples.

Apples (any crisp, firm variety) **2**
Unsalted butter **2 tablespoons**

1. Core the apples, but do not peel them. Cut them into quarters and then slice them wafer thin (use a mandoline if you have one).

2. Melt the butter in a skillet over medium to high heat. Add the apples and sauté until translucent.

PEACHES FOSTER STUFFING

There's just a hint of shiny in this stuffing—modeled on the sauce for Bananas Foster—since most of the alcohol cooks off in the skillet. If you prefer the traditional flavors, substitute two bananas for the peaches, and slice them into ½-inch-thick rounds.

> Peaches, ripe **2**
> Unsalted butter **2 ounces (½ stick)**
> Nutmeg, freshly ground **1 teaspoon**
> Dark rum **2 tablespoons (optional)**

1. Remove the pits from the peaches and slice the fruit into ½-inch-thick wedges.

2. Melt the butter in a large skillet over medium heat. Add the peaches and sauté until soft; don't overcook or they'll get mushy. Add the nutmeg and rum, if using, just before removing from the heat.

FRENCH TOAST BREAD PUDDING

Don't let the opportunity to serve a wonderful breakfast pass just because you don't want to stand by the stove. Tear up the bread and bake everything at one time, and it's essentially a bread pudding. **Serves a hungry group of 6.**

1. Preheat the oven to 300°F and place a rack in the middle. Following the proportions of the main recipe on page 19, tear the bread into 2-inch cubes and place them in a large bowl.

2. Add the milk, eggs, cinnamon, and vanilla and toss to combine. Fold in any of the Stuffed French Toast fillings, if you like, then mix in 1 cup superfine sugar and ¼ cup maple syrup.

3. Butter a deep 9-by-13 casserole dish and lightly sprinkle it with superfine sugar. Pour in the bread mixture and sprinkle turbinado sugar and cinnamon across the top. Bake until the pudding is set and the bread pieces don't jiggle, about 50 minutes.

For a dramatic presentation, serve French Toast Bread Pudding in a trifle bowl with heaps of berries, pillows of whipped cream, and pools of maple syrup.

POUND CAKE FRENCH TOAST

Bring this to the table and then stand back so you don't get crushed by the stampede! Grab a pound cake and try this—it'll knock you slap happy. Yes, cake for breakfast is outrageous, but I hear about it from a lot of people who come to CakeLove.

Refrigerate the pound cake ahead of time to make the slices good and firm before pan-frying. Turn them gently, because they become very fragile while bubbling in butter and oil. Maple syrup or jam pair well, but I couldn't believe how good this tasted with the Cream Cheese Drizzle (page 50).

Pound cake, very cold	1 loaf
Milk	2 cups
Eggs	3
Vanilla extract	1 teaspoon
Ground cinnamon	½ teaspoon
Unsalted butter or vegetable oil	up to ½ stick (¼ cup)

1. Place a large skillet on the stove over medium heat and preheat the oven to 275°F to keep the finished French toast warm.

2. Cut the pound cake into 2-inch-thick slices.

3. In a large casserole dish, whisk together the milk, eggs, vanilla, and cinnamon.

4. Soak each slice of pound cake for about 20 seconds, without flipping, in the milk mixture. Avoid oversaturating or the slice will fall apart in the pan.

5. Place enough of the butter in the skillet to thoroughly coat the bottom to prevent sticking. Place the soaked cake slice in the pan and cook until firmed.

6. Flip using a thin metal offset spatula and cook on the opposite side until lightly browned and crisped on the edges.

7. Serve immediately or hold on a heat-resistant plate in the warmed oven. Top with Cream Cheese Drizzle (page 50), if desired.

PANCAKES

Griddle cakes, flapjacks, pancakes—no matter what they're called, they mean one thing to me—a morning party! Pancakes make me giddy. Just like most of you, I grew up eating pancakes from a boxed mix that doubled as a biscuit mix. I loved it at the time, but now all my pancakes are made from scratch, and I've found that flapjacks are a great way to enjoy the textures and flavors of whole grains such as wheat, corn, rye, millet, and flax.

DON'T FULLY COMBINE the liquid ingredients into the flour mix—a few dry patches are ideal. Undermixing the batter keeps the pancakes light and airy.

LET THE BATTER REST for a few minutes after you've mixed it. This gives the gluten a chance to develop, and your pancakes will rise even more while cooking.

IT'S REALLY IMPORTANT to have the griddle at the right temp—hot enough to make you move your hand away if held there for about five seconds.

IN GENERAL, pancakes are ready to flip when bubbles appear across the top surface, usually about three to four minutes in.

USE PLENTY OF BUTTER or vegetable oil, or a combination of both. Pancakes tend to stick, so make sure the pan is well greased and hot. The batter should sizzle when it hits the surface!

A ¼-CUP MEASURE of batter should yield a pretty consistent 4-inch pancake. I use an old-fashioned ice-cream scoop with a trigger for easy portioning and to keep it nice and round.

TRADITIONAL PANCAKES

Yummy and delicious, these are the pancakes that come to mind when we think of the picture-perfect stack of flapjacks. When they're ready to flip, loads of bubbles form on top and the edges appear a bit drier. You can also check whether a pancake is ready to flip by lifting an edge to make sure it's a nice golden brown.

1. Preheat the oven to 275°F to keep the finished pancakes warm.

2. In a small bowl, combine the milk and lemon juice and set aside for 5 minutes to thicken. Add the egg, stirring it gently to break the yolk.

3. Meanwhile, in a medium bowl, combine the flour, sugar, baking powder, baking soda, and salt, and gently whisk for 10 seconds to combine. Set aside.

4. Gently fold the liquid ingredients into the flour mixture, but don't fully combine. It's always better to undermix; dry patches are okay. Let the batter rest for about 5 minutes.

5. Meanwhile, heat a large skillet or griddle over medium heat. When the surface is hot, add the butter or vegetable oil to coat.

6. Using a ¼-cup measure, drop 4 to 6 pancakes into the pan. Flip when bubbles appear, after 3 to 4 minutes.

7. Cook for another minute, then remove the pancakes to a heat-resistant plate in the warmed oven until ready to serve. Top with butter and maple syrup, as desired.

Milk	1 cup
Fresh lemon juice	¼ cup
Egg	1
Unbleached all-purpose flour	1 cup
Sugar	3 tablespoons
Baking powder	2¼ teaspoons
Baking soda	½ teaspoon
Salt	pinch
Butter or vegetable oil	1 tablespoon

SEE HOW THEY RISE

Here's a brief science lesson about what happens when the batter hits the griddle: You have to grease the griddle well because there is very little fat present in the batter itself. The protein in the grains provides structure and some height for our pancakes. When the batter is mixed, the liquid swells up the starch granules and weighs them down. Adding fat to the batter rather than the pan would weaken the structure even further and give us a very flat flapjack—otherwise known as a crepe.

CHOCOLATE PANCAKES

Whole rolled oats	⅔ cup
Pecans, roasted and hand crushed	¼ cup
Flaxseeds	1½ teaspoons
Sea salt	¼ teaspoon
Whole-wheat flour	½ cup
Turbinado sugar	1½ tablespoons
Millet meal	1 tablespoon
Cornmeal	1½ teaspoons
Baking powder	1⅛ teaspoons
Baking soda	¼ teaspoon
Chocolate chips or chunks	½ cup
Soy milk	1 cup
Fresh lemon juice	2 tablespoons
Egg	1
Canola oil	2 tablespoons, plus 2 teaspoons (optional)

None of my recipes will give you griddle cakes that puff very high. They're not crepes, but they won't cast a long shadow, either.

This recipe debuted at a party where my wife and I introduced our baby to our neighbors and close friends. Some of our guests had lactose allergies, so I wanted to prepare something just for them. Light, fluffy, and delicious, these pancakes lend themselves to tasty variations that bring a distinctive edge to any breakfast. (I used a mildly bittersweet 58% cacao bar for these, and each bite was chocolatey and delicious!)

1. Preheat the oven to 275°F to keep the finished pancakes warm.

2. Grind the oats, 1 tablespoon of the pecans, the flaxseeds, and salt to a powder in a spice grinder. Place the ground meal in a large bowl with the flour, sugar, millet, cornmeal, baking powder, baking soda, and chocolate. Whisk to combine and set aside.

3. Combine the soy milk and lemon juice in a bowl and let it stand for 5 minutes. Add the egg, stirring it gently to break the yolk, and 2 teaspoons of the canola oil, if using.

4. Gently fold the liquid ingredients into the flour mixture, but don't fully combine. Let the batter rest for 10 minutes.

5. Meanwhile, heat a large skillet or griddle over medium heat. When the skillet is hot, add 1 to 2 tablespoons of the oil, enough so it runs fast and leaves trails across the pan.

6. Using a ¼-cup measure, drop 4 to 6 pancakes into the pan. Flip when bubbles appear, about 4 minutes.

7. Cook for another minute, then remove the pancakes to a heat-resistant plate in the warmed oven.

Bacon-Chocolate Banana
Sandwich (page 30)

BACON-CHOCOLATE VARIATION

To the dry ingredients, add 4 to 5 slices crisp-cooked bacon, cooled and chopped into ¼-inch bits (about ½ cup).

BACON-CHOCOLATE BANANA SANDWICHES

Preheat the oven to 325°F and line a baking sheet with parchment paper. Make the Bacon-Chocolate Pancake Variation as directed, holding the finished pancakes on the prepared baking sheet. Slice 2 or 3 bananas in half lengthwise and, in a small pan, sauté them in a healthy amount of unsalted butter over low heat until lightly caramelized. Cut the banana halves to size for layering on the pancakes. Meanwhile, grate a bar of semi-sweet chocolate on the large holes of a box grater. To make the sandwiches, sprinkle 1 pancake with chocolate, layer on banana slices, sprinkle more chocolate, and then top with another pancake. Heat in the oven until the chocolate has melted, about 5 minutes. Devour these with glee and don't forget to have a napkin handy to wipe the gooey chocolate from the corners of your mouth!

MULTIGRAIN PANCAKES

Although my baking recipes typically feature unbleached, all-purpose flour, I prefer whole grains for pancakes. They not only taste better and have a lighter texture, but I find them easier to digest. Millet delivers a lot of flavor without much heft, and potato starch gives a light sweetness that complements the maple or honey.

In most recipes, cream of tartar is used in a 2-to-1 ratio with baking soda, but lemon juice reacts with the soda as well, releasing the gas that creates the bubbles that tell you it's time to flip the pancake.

Milk or soy milk	1 cup
Fresh lemon juice	2 tablespoons
Egg	1
Whole rolled oats	⅓ cup
Flaxseeds	2 teaspoons
Whole-wheat flour	½ cup
Millet flour	3 tablespoons
Superfine sugar	3 tablespoons
Potato starch	1 tablespoon
Cornmeal	1 tablespoon
Baking soda	¾ teaspoon
Cream of tartar	¾ teaspoon
Vegetable oil	1 to 2 tablespoons

1. Preheat the oven to 275°F to keep the finished pancakes warm.

2. In a small bowl, combine the milk and lemon juice and set aside for 5 minutes to thicken. Add the egg, stirring it gently to break the yolk.

3. Meanwhile, mill the oats and flaxseeds to a powder in a spice grinder. Whisk to combine them in a medium bowl with the whole-wheat and millet flours, sugar, potato starch, cornmeal, baking soda, and cream of tartar.

4. Gently stir the liquid ingredients into the flour mixture, but don't fully combine. Set aside for another 5 minutes.

5. Meanwhile, heat a large skillet or griddle over medium heat. When the skillet is hot, pour the vegetable oil onto the griddle and spread it out.

6. Using a ¼-cup measure, drop 4 to 6 pancakes into the pan. Flip when bubbles appear, after 3 to 4 minutes.

7. Cook for another minute, then remove the pancakes to a heat-resistant plate in the warmed oven until ready to serve. Top with butter and maple syrup, as desired.

DOUBLE-DUTY WARMING
Preheat the oven when you begin to mix your batter. Not only will it keep the first batches warm, but you can place your syrup on the stovetop and let the radiant heat bring the syrup up to a lovely warm temperature.

COCONUT MILK FLAPJACKS

Banana, mashed	1 cup (about 6 ounces)
Coconut milk or milk	1 cup
Egg	1
Fresh lemon juice	2 tablespoons
Honey	2 teaspoons
Vanilla extract	1 teaspoon
Whole-wheat flour	1 cup
Whole rolled oats	¼ cup
Buckwheat flour	2 tablespoons
Superfine sugar	1 tablespoon
Baking powder	1½ teaspoons
Baking soda	½ teaspoon
Salt	¼ teaspoon
Butter or vegetable oil	1 tablespoon
Cinnamon and allspice	to sprinkle

The coconut milk in these delicious griddle cakes will bring a taste of the Caribbean to even the coldest winter mornings. The bouquet of island flavor comes alive with the allspice and coconut milk.

1. Preheat the oven to 275°F to keep the finished pancakes warm.

2. Combine the banana in a medium bowl with the coconut milk, egg, lemon juice, honey, and vanilla extract. Set aside for 5 minutes.

3. In a large bowl, whisk to combine the whole-wheat flour, oats, buckwheat flour, sugar, baking powder, baking soda, and salt.

4. Gently fold the liquid ingredients into the flour mixture, but don't fully combine. Let the batter rest for 10 minutes to soften the oats.

5. Meanwhile, heat a large skillet or griddle over medium heat. When the surface is hot, add the butter or vegetable oil and spread it out.

6. Using a ¼-cup measure, drop 4 to 6 pancakes into the pan. Flip when bubbles appear, after about 3 to 4 minutes.

7. Cook for another minute, then remove the pancakes to a heat-resistant plate in the warmed oven.

8. Sprinkle with a dusting of cinnamon and allspice and serve with warmed maple syrup or try topping with Raspberry Compote (page 51).

Pancakes are always best served warm, so preheat the oven to hold the first ones while you're making the rest. I keep mine at about 275°F.

Coconut Milk Flapacks with
Raspberry Compote (page 51)

BLUEBERRY PANCAKES

Unbleached all-purpose flour	1½ cups
Confectioners' sugar	2 tablespoons
Superfine sugar	2 tablespoons
Cornmeal	1 tablespoon
Baking powder	1 tablespoon
Salt	½ teaspoon
Milk	1½ cups
Egg	1
Vanilla extract	1 teaspoon
Fresh blueberries	1 cup
Butter or vegetable oil	1 tablespoon

It doesn't hurt to make one "practice pancake" before forging ahead with a whole griddle full of hotcakes. Every batter behaves differently, and there's not a lot of room for error once the cooking starts.

Blueberry pancakes rank high on my list of favorite things. Big splotches of blueberries deep inside extra-large griddlecakes, dripping butter and oozing pure maple syrup . . . now we're talking about Sunday morning bliss! The blueberry seems to have been made for the pancake, but there are other, equally delicious substitutes: Whole raspberries, sliced strawberries, or even thin apple slices (less than ¼ inch thick) are all good. Just keep the quantities consistent.

   This is a very lumpy batter, but it makes a puffy pancake that hugs the berries well. Gently fold in the wet ingredients; you don't need to keep stirring until the batter is smooth.

1. Preheat the oven to 275°F to keep the finished pancakes warm.

2. In a large bowl, combine the flour, sugars, cornmeal, baking powder, and salt. Gently whisk for 10 seconds to combine. Set aside.

3. In another bowl, combine the milk, egg, and vanilla.

4. Gently fold the liquid ingredients into the flour mixture, but don't fully combine. Just as gently fold in the blueberries. It's always better to undermix; dry patches are ideal. Let the batter rest for about 3 minutes.

5. Meanwhile, heat a large skillet or griddle over medium heat. When the surface is hot, add the butter or vegetable oil to coat. Use more if necessary—the berries have a tendency to stick.

6. Using a ¼-cup measure, drop 4 to 6 pancakes into the pan. Flip when bubbles appear, after about 3 to 4 minutes.

7. Cook for another minute, then remove the pancakes to a heat-resistant plate in the warmed oven. Top with butter and maple syrup, as desired.

BUCKWHEAT PANCAKES

Milk or soy milk	1 cup plus 2 tablespoons
Fresh lemon juice	4 to 6 tablespoons
Egg	1
Vanilla extract	1 teaspoon (optional)
Whole-wheat flour, sifted	1 cup
Buckwheat flour	½ cup
Whole rolled oats	¼ cup
Superfine sugar	2 tablespoons
Baking powder	1 teaspoon
Baking soda	1 teaspoon
Salt	½ teaspoon
Butter or vegetable oil	1 tablespoon

When I was a little boy, my dad made pancakes for our family on Sunday mornings. It was always fun to see Dad in the kitchen, and my sisters and I always looked forward to those special mornings. A health-minded physician, Pops's pancakes didn't come from a box. He whipped up a number of different recipes, but one that stayed in my mind is for buckwheat pancakes. They're a little different from regular pancakes, but the flavor and texture is a nice change of pace—and perfect for special Sunday mornings.

1. Preheat the oven to 275°F to keep the finished pancakes warm.

2. In a small bowl, combine the milk and lemon juice. Set aside for 5 minutes. Add the egg and vanilla (if using), stirring gently to break the yolk.

3. In a large bowl, combine the flours, oats, sugar, baking powder, baking soda, and salt. Whisk for 10 seconds to combine.

4. Gently fold the liquid ingredients into the flour mixture, but don't fully combine. Set aside for 3 to 5 minutes.

5. Meanwhile, heat a large skillet or griddle over medium heat. When the surface is hot, add the butter or vegetable oil.

6. Using a ¼-cup measure, drop 4 to 6 pancakes into the pan. Flip when bubbles appear, after 3 to 4 minutes.

7. Cook for another minute, then remove the pancakes to a heat-resistant plate in the warmed oven. Top with butter and maple syrup, as desired.

BANANA PANCAKES

Banana pancakes are always a special treat. I'll only use bananas with soft yellow skin—no green streaks and no brown spots. Once cooked, the fruit gets really, really hot, so let these pancakes cool a bit before you dig in.

Rye may seem like an odd addition, but pancakes made with more than one type of flour carry a greater depth of flavor.

Milk or soy milk	1 cup plus 2 tablespoons
Fresh lemon juice	4 to 6 tablespoons
Egg	1
Whole rolled oats	½ cup
Whole-wheat flour	¾ cup
Unbleached all-purpose flour	¼ cup
Rye flour	1 tablespoon
Turbinado sugar	2 tablespoons
Cornmeal	1 tablespoon
Baking powder	2 teaspoons
Lemon zest	1 teaspoon
Nutmeg, freshly grated	½ teaspoon
Sea salt	¼ teaspoon
Banana	1 medium
Butter or vegetable oil	1 tablespoon

1. Preheat the oven to 275°F to keep the finished pancakes warm.

2. In a small bowl, combine the milk and lemon juice. Set aside for 5 minutes. Add the egg, stirring it gently to break the yolk.

3. Grind the oats into a fine powder using a spice grinder.

4. In a large bowl, combine the ground oats with the flours, sugar, cornmeal, baking powder, lemon zest, nutmeg, and salt. Whisk for 10 seconds to thoroughly combine.

5. Peel and slice the banana into ¼-inch slices and toss to combine with the flour mixture. Set aside.

6. Gently stir the liquids into the flour mixture, but don't fully combine. Set aside for 3 to 5 minutes.

7. Meanwhile, heat a large skillet or griddle over medium heat. When the surface is hot, add the butter or vegetable oil.

8. Using a ¼-cup measure, drop 4 to 6 pancakes into the pan. Flip when bubbles appear, after 3 to 4 minutes.

9. Cook for another minute, then remove the pancakes to a heat-resistant plate in the warmed oven. Top with butter and maple syrup, as desired.

WAFFLES

I love waffles because the ingredients and techniques used are so similar to cake baking—it's like a mini focus lab for experimenting with flavor combinations. The goal here is to serve fluffy waffles that are crispy on the outside and soft in the middle. Allow one to two waffles per serving, depending on the amount of toppings added and individual appetites. Heat the waffle iron now, because a whole bunch of tempting options are waiting!

USE A STAND MIXER to beat the egg whites and whip the batter. It will make the job at hand much easier.

HAVE ALL YOUR INGREDIENTS at room temperature, then let the finished batter sit for at least 10 minutes before beginning to cook.

DON'T LADLE cold waffle batter into a hot waffle iron or it'll stick, even if you've used nonstick spray on a nonstick cooking surface.

DON'T FILL the wells of the waffle iron completely—when you press down the lid, the batter will be pushed beyond the edges.

PECAN WAFFLES

In 2004, I was vacationing with my family in West Palm Beach, Florida. Our week of R&R was cut short by an inky sky, swift waves, and mandatory evacuation due to the approach of Hurricane Frances. Racing ahead of the storm, we criss-crossed central Florida, realizing along the way that the memorable part of our vacation would be this zany car ride.

My sister Liz drove the night shift and pulled off at a roadside restaurant just north of the Georgia state line at daybreak. Everyone ordered the same thing—pecan waffles—and no one made a peep once they were served. We just sat there, eating silently and smiling at our luck.

Eggs, separated	2
Superfine sugar	4 tablespoons
Milk	1½ cups
Unsalted butter, melted	2 tablespoons
Vanilla extract	1 teaspoon
Rum	1 teaspoon
Pecans, roasted	6 ounces, divided
Confectioners' sugar	⅔ cup
Unbleached all-purpose or pastry flour	7½ ounces (1½ cups)
Baking powder	2 teaspoons
Salt	1 teaspoon

1. Start the waffle iron and preheat the oven to 200°F to keep the finished waffles warm.

2. In the bowl of a stand mixer fitted with the whisk attachment, whip the egg whites to stiff peaks, then sprinkle in 2 tablespoons of the superfine sugar with the mixer on high speed. Move the meringue to a separate bowl and set aside.

3. Using the same bowl and whisk, mix the egg yolks and the remaining 2 tablespoons superfine sugar on high speed for 30 seconds. Reduce the speed to medium and add the milk, butter, vanilla, and rum.

4. Meanwhile, grind half of the pecans and all of the confectioners' sugar in a food processor into a fine powder. Whisk to combine them with the flour, baking powder, and salt in a large bowl. Fold the flour mixture into the yolk base, then gently fold in the meringue.

5. Spray the waffle iron with plenty of nonstick spray. Ladle ¼ cup batter onto each square of the iron. Sprinkle on a small handful of the remaining roasted pecans.

6. Cook following the waffle iron's directions. Serve immediately or hold on a heat-resistant plate in the warmed oven.

Roast and cool the pecans ahead of time before grinding them with the confectioners' sugar. Pecans contain a lot of oil and trying to grind warm ones will result in a bit of a mess.

FRIED CHICKEN & WAFFLES

For a whole lot of folks, there's no better pairing for waffles than fried chicken! I'm a latecomer to this tradition, but it wins Best in Taste, hands down. When you get a bite of crispy skin, succulent meat, fluffy waffles, and sweet, dripping syrup all in one mouthful, you'll be a convert, too!

1. In a large vessel, combine the milk and lemon juice and add the chicken parts. Marinate it in the fridge for 2 to 4 hours. Remove the chicken from the marinade, shake off the excess, and bring it to room temperature.

2. Pour the oil into a deep frying pan and heat over medium to high heat until it registers 350°F on a deep-fry thermometer. Preheat the oven to 250°F to keep the finished chicken warm prior to serving.

3. Crack the eggs into a large bowl and whisk to scramble.

4. In a large container with a lid, combine the flour, pepper, onion powder, salt, garlic powder, paprika, thyme, and sugar.

5. Working with one piece at a time, dip the chicken in the eggs, then dredge it in the flour mixture by covering the container and shaking vigorously to make sure that the chicken is well coated. For extra-crispy chicken, re-dip the chicken in the eggs and dredge again.

6. Make sure the chicken is totally covered in flour mix before carefully submerging it into the oil. Cook one piece at a time until it floats and is golden brown all over.

7. Remove and drain the chicken on oil-absorbent paper and hold it on a heat-resistant plate in the warmed oven while you make the Vanilla Waffles.

8. For each serving, plate 2 pieces of chicken alongside 2 waffles topped with butter and warm maple syrup, as desired.

Milk	1 quart
Fresh lemon juice	¼ cup
Whole chicken, cut up	1 (3-pound) bird
Vegetable oil	1 to 2 quarts
Eggs	4
Unbleached all-purpose flour	3 cups
Freshly ground black pepper	1 tablespoon
Onion powder	1 tablespoon
Sea salt	1 tablespoon
Garlic powder	2 teaspoons
Paprika	2 teaspoons
Fresh thyme	2 teaspoons
Sugar	½ teaspoon
Vanilla Waffles (page 42)	1 recipe

Don't fry cold chicken—cold chicken means cold bones, which slow the cooking process. It will take too long to cook and the skin will burn before the meat is done.

VANILLA WAFFLES

Eggs, separated	2
Superfine sugar	4 tablespoons
Half-and-half	1¼ cups
Unsalted butter, melted	2 tablespoons
Vanilla extract	1 teaspoon
Unbleached all-purpose flour	5 ounces (1 cup)
Baking powder	2 teaspoons
Salt	½ teaspoon

There's nothing vanilla about this vanilla! This is a tasty basic waffle that will deliciously accommodate any number of toppings. A fun and low-fat way to make these (or any waffles) even more special is to make a "waffle cake" as shown in the photo opposite, stacking the waffles with Cooked Meringue Icing (page 167) in between.

1. Start the waffle iron and preheat the oven to 200°F to keep the finished waffles warm.

2. In the bowl of a stand mixer fitted with the whisk attachment, whip the egg whites to stiff peaks, then sprinkle in 2 tablespoons of the sugar with the mixer on high speed. Carefully move the meringue to a separate bowl and set aside.

3. Using the same bowl and whisk, mix the egg yolks and remaining 2 tablespoons sugar on high speed for 30 seconds. Reduce the speed to medium and add the half-and-half, butter, and vanilla.

4. Meanwhile, in another bowl, whisk to combine the flour, baking powder, and salt. Fold the flour mixture into the yolk base, then gently fold in the meringue.

5. Spray the waffle iron with plenty of nonstick spray. Ladle ¼ cup batter onto each square of the iron.

6. Cook following the waffle iron's directions. Serve immediately or hold on a heat-resistant plate in the warmed oven.

Vanilla Waffle Cake
with Cooked Meringue
Icing (page 167)

WHITE-CHOCOLATE WAFFLES

My wife's favorite snack is little bits of white chocolate—I've caught her sneaking some at 8 A.M.! So this recipe is for her, for when she wants her white-chocolate fix for breakfast. It's important to warm all of the ingredients so the white chocolate won't stiffen and clump up. Anything cold will harden the cocoa butter and ruin the texture. Bittersweet chocolate pieces work just as well if you favor dark chocolate.

Eggs	4
Superfine sugar	6 tablespoons
Half-and-half	1¼ cups
Vanilla extract	1 teaspoon
White chocolate, melted	3 to 4 ounces (see Note)
Unbleached cake flour	7 ounces (1½ cups)
Baking powder	1 tablespoon
Salt	¼ teaspoon

1. Start the waffle iron and preheat the oven to 200°F to keep the finished waffles warm.

2. Run warm water over the eggs for 20 seconds, then separate them. In the bowl of a stand mixer fitted with the whisk attachment, whip the egg whites to stiff peaks, then sprinkle in 4 tablespoons of the sugar with the mixer on high speed. Carefully move the meringue to a separate bowl and set aside.

3. Using the same bowl and whisk, mix the yolks and the remaining 2 tablespoons sugar on high speed for 30 seconds. Reduce the speed to medium and add the half-and-half and vanilla.

4. Scrape the melted white chocolate into the mixer and whip to incorporate.

5. Meanwhile, in another bowl, whisk the flour, baking powder, and salt to combine. Fold the flour mixture into the yolk base, then gently fold in the meringue.

6. Spray the waffle iron with plenty of nonstick spray. Ladle ¼ cup batter onto each square of the iron.

7. Cook following the waffle iron's directions. Serve immediately or hold on a heat-resistant plate in the warmed oven.

NOTE:
Melt white chocolate in a double-boiler or a metal bowl placed over a saucepan of steaming water.

ON THE TOP:
FLAVORED BUTTERS, SYRUPS, AND DRIZZLES

I slather biscuits with sweet butter and scones with jams and preserves, drizzle coffee cakes and rolls with glazes and sweet icings, and always—always—serve pancakes with syrup! Here's my take on a few classic toppings that can perform in concert with a variety of recipes throughout the book.

MAPLE SYRUP

Maple syrup—the concentrated tree sap of the sugar maple tree—is my preferred choice for pancakes. My mother always insisted on pure maple syrup in our house, and the tradition continues with my family. Maple syrup comes in a range of grades (and different countries and even different states have their own grading systems). In most of the United States, Grade A is divided into three categories: Light, Medium, and Dark Amber; Grade B is darker than Grade A Dark Amber. I prefer Grade A Light Amber for everything, whether I'm enjoying pancakes or using the syrup as an ingredient (you can always find me adding it to butternut squash). A lot of bakers will opt for Grade B for baking because it's more concentrated, but I just prefer to keep one style in my pantry. No matter which grade you choose, please use real maple syrup. The commercial alternatives are simply artificially flavored corn syrup, and there's just no comparison when it comes to the taste.

Making maple syrup is a time-intensive labor of love. Tree sap from the sugar maple is harvested in a few short weeks every spring when days are warm and nights are cold. The sap is boiled down 24 hours a day (before it goes rancid) to concentrate and develop it into a syrup. It takes 10 gallons of sap to produce 1 gallon of syrup—a long process that makes the sugar shack smell heavenly.

A fair amount of maple syrup is produced in northeast Ohio, where I grew up, and I fondly recall hauling buckets of sap during a few high school spring breaks. Carrying sap and helping boil down the syrup was one of the best hands-on lessons ever. It was magical to watch the sap become concentrated and sweeter. The color deepened as the sap moved from chamber to chamber over a roaring wood-burning fire. Tasting the first drips of a new batch of syrup is incomparable to just having it warmed and poured over pancakes. There's something about the smell of the burning timbers, the exhaustion from moving equipment, and the burst of flavor from something plain transformed into sweet heat that makes a lasting impression. I'm agog for maple!

OTHER NATURAL SWEETENERS

Maple sugars are available in various granulations; a perfect substitute for refined sugar that will add a great mapley flavor. Large grains are very tasty in spice blends and on sugar-cured meat and fish.

Birch syrup, made from the sap of birch trees, tastes a lot like maple syrup, but is not quite as sweet.

Agave nectar (or syrup) is produced from the sap of the agave plant. Both light and dark versions are available: The light has a taste closer to honey; the dark, which is simply a less-filtered version, is closer to maple syrup. The carbohydrate in agave nectar has a low glycemic index, making it a natural option for people who need to manage their blood sugar.

Cane syrup is reduced sugarcane juice, but it's often marketed in the form of a thick and dark syrup with a strong flavor.

Treacle, as it's most commonly known in Great Britain, is a by-product of sugar refining. Two types are available: dark treacle, which is most similar to molasses, and light treacle (also called golden syrup), which is more refined.

Raw honey is part of an entire galaxy of honeys available beyond the simple clover variety we all grew up with. Just like wine, honey has its own form of *terroir* and will take on the subtle flavor of whatever type of plant the bees have been visiting for pollen. So explore the range available at your grocer or specialty shop, from orange blossom to Tupelo, or seek out a honey purveyor at your local farmers market. The differences will wake up your taste buds and infuse your recipes with a new energy.

Creamed honey, also called whipped honey or honey butter, is raw honey that has gone through a controlled crystallization process. It is creamy in texture and can be spread like softened butter.

BUTTER

My go-to butter is standard American unsalted butter. As I said earlier, if you like the way it tastes on your toast, then that's the butter you should use. Do pay attention to the expiration date, as unsalted butter has a shorter shelf life than salted. Always buy the freshest butter you can find. Butters from Ireland and continental Europe—and domestic butters made in the European style— have a delicate flavor and a much higher fat content than our supermarket brands. They work well for pan-frying but will yield heavier results in baked goods.

FLAVORED BUTTERS

Any sweet or savory flavoring can be added to butter, bringing a new taste to baked goods as well as ramping up the flavor profile of a sizzling steak or broiled fish fillet. In fact, making flavored butter is a great way to use up leftover fresh herbs or surplus dried spices. Once mixed, you can store the butter logs in the freezer for months.

Here are recipes for three of my favorite flavored butters. The Herbed Butter is a sweet and savory spread that goes well with any of the multigrain pancakes because it's such a nice contrast of flavors. It's unusual, I know, but I like bold, stand-out flavors. The Jalapeño-Honey Butter is a really wild blend of flavors that's perfect for melting on anything served warm. It's sweet and only mildly spicy. I especially love it with Quick Home-Spun Cornbread (page 144) but you can also pair it with pancakes, scones, or muffins when you're looking to add flavor and color to the plate. And, Honey Butter—well it works on just about everything.

HERBED BUTTER

Makes ¾ cup

Unsalted butter, lightly chilled **4 ounces (1 stick)**

Fresh marjoram **1 tablespoon**

Fresh cilantro **1 tablespoon**

Honey (raw or creamed) **2 teaspoons**

Fresh thyme, chopped **1 teaspoon**

Sugar **1 teaspoon**

Lemon zest **½ teaspoon**

Kosher salt **½ teaspoon**

Ground dried rosemary **¼ teaspoon**

Freshly ground black pepper **¼ teaspoon**

1. Add all of the ingredients to the work bowl of a food processor fitted with the steel blade. Pulse 10 to 15 times to combine. Add a few drops of water if the spread is too thick and won't combine.

2. Use a flexible spatula to remove the butter from the work bowl and mold it into a log using plastic wrap. Refrigerate or freeze until needed.

HONEY BUTTER

Makes ½ cup

Unsalted butter **1 stick**

Raw honey **1 to 2 tablespoons**

Sea salt **¼ teaspoon**

1. Whip all ingredients in a food processor or mixer until smooth.

2. Use a flexible spatula to remove the butter from the work bowl and mold it into a log using plastic wrap. Refrigerate or freeze until needed.

JALAPEÑO-HONEY BUTTER

Makes ¾ cup

Jalapeño pepper, seeds and ribs removed **1**

Garlic clove, pressed **1**

Unsalted butter, softened **5 ounces (1¼ sticks)**

Fresh cilantro, chopped **2 tablespoons**

Honey **2 tablespoons**

Garlic cloves, peeled **2**

Superfine sugar **2 teaspoons**

Lemon or lime zest **1 tablespoon**

Vanilla extract **¼ teaspoon**

Salt **a pinch**

Freshly ground black pepper **a pinch**

Hot sauce **2 shakes**

1. In a small pan over medium heat, quickly sauté the jalapeño and pressed garlic in 1 tablespoon of the butter. Cool to room temperature before proceeding.

2. Add the jalapeño-garlic mixture, along with all the remaining ingredients, to the work bowl of a food processor fitted with the steel blade. Pulse 10 to 15 times to combine. Add a few drops of water if the spread is too thick and won't combine.

3. Use a flexible spatula to remove the butter from the work bowl and mold it into a log using plastic wrap. Refrigerate or freeze until needed.

DRIZZLES AND GLAZES

Icing for breakfast or brunch is a little over the top, but no one will stop you once they taste it. These simple glazes bring that finishing hit of sugar to muffins, scones, quick breads, and cakes. Drizzle any of these over French toast and stand back!

CREAM CHEESE DRIZZLE

A great multipurpose drizzle that will pour easily from a spoon, this recipe makes enough to cover nine muffins, with plenty left over for topping other goodies.

Makes 2 cups

Unsalted butter, softened **3 tablespoons**

Cream cheese, softened **2 ounces (¼ cup)**

Confectioners' sugar **1 cup, sifted**

Milk **¾ cup**

Vanilla extract **1 teaspoon**

Sea salt **tiny pinch**

1. In the bowl of a stand mixer fitted with the paddle attachment, beat the butter until smooth. Add the cream cheese and continue to beat on medium speed until very smooth.

2. Add the sugar, milk, vanilla, and salt, and beat on low until smooth.

3. Drizzle on your baked goods as desired. Store the extra icing in an airtight container in the refrigerator for up to 1 week.

CINNAMON-SUGAR GLAZE

Makes 1¼ cup

> Confectioners' sugar 1 cup, sifted, plus extra as needed
>
> Milk 1 to 2 tablespoons
>
> Ground cinnamon ½ teaspoon
>
> Vanilla extract ½ teaspoon
>
> Salt a pinch
>
> Ground allspice a pinch (optional)

1. Combine all the ingredients in a medium bowl and stir with a whisk or fork until smooth. Add more sugar, if needed, to thicken the glaze to a desired consistency.

2. Use to glaze cakes or quick breads, or store in an airtight container in the refrigerator for up to 1 week.

LEMON GLAZE

Makes ½ cup

> Confectioners' sugar ½ cup, sifted, plus extra as needed
>
> Fresh lemon juice 1 tablespoon

1. Combine the sugar and juice in a small bowl and stir until smooth. Add more sugar, if needed, to thicken the glaze to a desired consistency.

2. Use to glaze cakes and quick breads, or store in an airtight container in the refrigerator for up to 1 week.

ORANGE GLAZE

Makes 2 cups

> Confectioners' sugar 2 cups, sifted, plus extra as needed
>
> Fresh orange juice 2 to 4 tablespoons
>
> Vanilla extract ½ teaspoon

1. Combine the ingredients in a medium bowl and stir until smooth. Add more sugar, if needed, to thicken the glaze to a desired consistency.

2. Use to glaze cakes or quick breads, or store in an airtight container in the refrigerator for up to 1 week.

RASPBERRY COMPOTE

Makes 1 cup

> Raspberries 1 pint
>
> Sugar ¼ cup
>
> Fresh lemon juice 1 tablespoon

1. Combine all the ingredients in a heavy-bottomed saucepan over medium heat and bring to a simmer, about 5 to 7 minutes.

2. Immediately remove the pan from the heat and pour the compote into a heatproof container.

EGGS, FRITTATAS, AND QUICHES

Plain or fancy, eggs are the perfect breakfast food, and once you've mastered a well-cooked egg, you'll have any number of tasty creations at your fingertips. Eggs are delicious alone or as the basis for more complex creations like frittatas and quiches.

EGGS

Does anything say "breakfast" more than an egg? I love eggs and am always surprised at how much I crave such a common food. But what I like most about them is their versatility—everything about the egg experience depends on how it's prepared, and each cooking method results in a different texture and flavor. Eggs offer so much variety that we never get tired of them.

DEPENDING ON THE APPETITE and the preparation, I serve one to two eggs per person.

I TEND TO reduce the heat once I flip or stir the eggs in the pan. As they cook, they need less heat, so I oblige and lower the flame.

SERVE 'EM HOT! No one wants lukewarm eggs. Some dishes will hold in the oven or can be reheated, but all eggs will look and taste better served right off the stove or hot from the oven.

CRACK EGGS into a bowl rather than directly into the pan. That way, any stray pieces of shell are easily removed.

EGGS WILL KEEP COOKING once they've left the pan, and overcooked eggs can be rubbery and just plain unappealing. So pull them off the heat while they're still a little undercooked.

SERVES 1

MY FRIED EGGS

Frying is one of the simplest ways to prepare eggs, but everyone likes theirs cooked a certain way. I like my yolk warm and a little runny. Toast with jam and some fried eggs is how I start my day a few times a week.

Unsalted butter	1 tablespoon or less
Kosher or sea salt	1 or 2 pinches
Eggs	2

1. Heat a medium (7-inch) skillet over medium heat.

2. Rub the pan with the butter to lightly to coat the surface. Once the butter melts, lightly sprinkle the surface with a pinch of salt.

3. Crack each egg into a bowl and slide it into the pan one at a time; avoid overlapping the egg whites. Sprinkle the eggs with another pinch of salt, if you wish.

4. When the whites begin to set, fill half an egg shell with water and pour the water into the pan at the edge. The eggs are ready to be gently flipped when the egg whites firm up and gain color with a touch of brown on the edge.

5. For a runny yolk, turn off the heat and allow the eggs to continue cooking with the radiant heat for about 20 seconds. For a firm yolk, continue cooking for another 20 seconds and then turn off the heat. Rest them in the pan for about 30 seconds, then remove to a plate.

WARM PLATES, HOT FOOD!

Cold plates draw heat away from your food, cooling it down more quickly. For food that tastes its best, warm your plates on the middle of the stovetop, next to the hot skillets, or in a low oven before serving.

SOFT-SCRAMBLED EGGS

Eggs	3
Unsalted butter	1 tablespoon
Olive oil	1 tablespoon
Kosher or sea salt	1 pinch

There's nothing sexy or gourmet about scrambled eggs, but few dishes have more universal appeal. A few simple tricks are the difference between good eggs and great ones.

Heat the pan and use a combination of unsalted butter and olive oil; together they add a nice flavor to the eggs. Add salt to the pan before adding the eggs—this way you can see how much you've used and you won't oversalt. Add a touch of water, not milk, when stirring the eggs in a bowl. Cook the eggs slowly over low heat, and move the eggs around the pan often. I think the texture is more interesting if the eggs are left a little undercooked, but some prefer a hard scramble.

SHORT ON TIME?

Microwave 'em in less than minute!

Lightly grease a microwave-safe ceramic or glass bowl with olive oil and butter, then sprinkle with a dash of salt.

Crack 2 eggs into the bowl and add 1 to 2 teaspoons water. Whisk or stir briskly with a fork to combine.

Microwave on full power for approximately 30 seconds.

Sprinkle with another dash of salt and serve.

1. Heat a medium (7-inch) skillet over low to medium heat.

2. Crack the eggs into a bowl and add 1 to 2 teaspoons water. Whisk or stir briskly with a fork until scrambled, then set aside.

3. Add the butter and oil to the pan to lightly coat the surface. Lightly sprinkle the salt in the pan.

4. Pour the eggs into the center of the pan and let them cook for about 30 seconds, then begin to gently push the eggs around the pan with a fork or spatula. Repeat about every 30 seconds.

5. For soft scrambled eggs, turn off the heat after about 3 to 4 minutes—the eggs will be creamy and still have liquid in them. For a harder scramble, continue cooking to desired doneness.

FIESTA EGGS

On a recent visit with my parents, I asked my dad if he wanted some eggs for breakfast. He said, "Sure, with peppers and onions." I was just going to make plain old scrambled eggs, but then I thought, "How many times do I get to make eggs for my dad?" Not nearly enough! I called these Fiesta Eggs because the diced peppers and onions reminded me of confetti, and suddenly a fairly typical morning was transformed into a memory. Life's a party when you treat it like one.

Olive oil	2 to 3 tablespoons
Yellow onion, diced	½
Orange bell pepper, diced	½
Red or green bell pepper, diced	½
Salt and freshly ground black pepper	to taste
Eggs	4

1. Heat a medium (7-inch) skillet over medium to high heat and add the oil.

2. Add the onion and peppers and sauté for 2 minutes. Add salt and pepper to taste.

3. Meanwhile, crack the eggs into a medium bowl. Add 2 tablespoons water and stir well to scramble.

4. Pour the eggs over the onion and peppers and let them cook for about 30 seconds, then begin to gently push the eggs around the pan with a fork or spatula. Repeat about every 30 seconds.

5. Turn off the heat, finish cooking in the pan, and serve hot.

POACHED EGGS

White vinegar or fresh lemon juice	1 tablespoon
Salt	½ teaspoon
Eggs	as needed

It's fairly easy to poach eggs for yourself or for a crowd when armed with the right technique and a few simple tools and ingredients. First, the water should be steaming, not simmering, in order to cook the whites without setting the yolk. Add a splash of white vinegar or lemon juice and a touch of salt to the water. The salt will add flavor and the acid will help set the protein and give shape to the white. Crack each egg into a bowl, gently stir the water to create a whirlpool in the pot, and then gently slide the egg into the center of the whirl. I poach my eggs one at a time. If you are cooking eggs for a crowd, hold them in an ice bath to stop the cooking process; then reheat them briefly as directed, right before serving.

1. Heat 1 quart water in a 7-inch sauté pan over medium heat so that it's steaming and producing small bubbles that slowly release from the bottom. The temperature should be about 175°F.

2. If you are cooking more than one egg, prepare a shallow ice bath in which to place the poached eggs in order to stop the cooking process.

3. Add the vinegar and salt to the water and gently swirl with the slotted spoon to create a whirlpool.

4. Working with one egg at a time, crack the egg into a small, shallow bowl.

5. Gently lower the egg into the pocket of the whirlpool. The egg should take shape within 10 to 15 seconds.

6. Cook for 3 to 4 minutes or up to 7 minutes if you want a firmer yolk. Gently release the egg from the bottom of the pan with a silicone spatula. If the egg releases on its own, it's ready to remove.

7. Remove the poached egg with a slotted spoon and transfer it to the ice bath or dab with a paper towel if serving immediately. (You can hold them in an ice bath for up to 24 hours if you're hosting a party.) Briefly return them to warm water with the slotted spoon to refresh them.

EGGS BENEDICT

Unsalted butter	3 ounces (¾ stick)
Heavy cream	¼ cup
Egg yolks	2, stirred
Fresh lemon juice	2 to 3 tablespoons
Sea salt	½ teaspoon
Poached Eggs (page 58)	4
Canadian bacon	4 pieces
English muffins	2

The classic brunch dish serves up poached eggs over an English muffin and bacon, topped with a rich hollandaise sauce. Canadian bacon is the traditional meat, but there's plenty of room for new pairings at my table. I like thick-cut smoked bacon—but you can also substitute cooked spinach instead of meat for Eggs Florentine. Poaching eggs for a crowd and making hollandaise are a bit involved, so practice before tackling this for your next brunch. Making the sauce isn't difficult, but it must be cooked in a double boiler or a heatproof bowl over simmering water; do not attempt it in a pan directly over the heat.

1. To make the hollandaise: Bring 1 inch of water to a simmer in a 2-quart saucepan.

2. In a heatproof bowl that nests on top of the pot but doesn't make contact with the water, melt 2 ounces of the butter, then add the cream. Whisk in the yolks and stir to prevent them from setting or starting to scramble. Stir in the lemon juice and salt. Cook, stirring constantly, until the sauce thickens.

3. Remove the hollandaise sauce from the heat and whisk briskly to increase the volume and lighten color. Serve immediately or hold briefly over lightly steaming water.

4. Prepare the poached eggs as directed.

5. In a separate 7-inch skillet, fry the bacon until lightly browned on both sides.

6. While the bacon cooks, split and toast the English muffins.

7. Butter the muffin halves and place one on each plate. Place a piece of bacon on each muffin, then a poached egg, followed by a ladleful of hollandaise sauce.

PERFECT HARD-BOILED EGGS

A firm, bright yellow yolk and soft white are the standard for a well-made hard-boiled egg. I find this is easily done if you immediately move it from the hot water directly into an ice bath until it's thoroughly chilled.

Eggs	6
Salt	2 tablespoons

1. Place the eggs on their sides in a pot and cover with cold water. Add salt, up to 2 tablespoons.

2. Place over medium to high heat and bring to a rolling boil. Boil for up to 8 minutes for small to large eggs or up to 10 minutes for extra-large or jumbo eggs.

3. Meanwhile, prepare an ice bath, leaving plenty of room for the eggs to float under the ice.

4. Carefully transfer the eggs to the ice bath with tongs.

5. Cool the eggs in the ice water for 15 to 20 minutes. Gently tap each egg against a hard surface to crack and remove the shell.

RED DEVILED EGGS

Hard-boiled eggs (see page 61)	6
Mayonnaise	2 tablespoons
Dijon mustard	1 teaspoon
White balsamic vinegar	1 teaspoon
Hot sauce (Tabasco)	1 teaspoon
Ground mustard	½ teaspoon
Sea salt	½ teaspoon, plus more for garnish
Ground white pepper	½ teaspoon
Smoked paprika	½ teaspoon, plus more for garnish
Cayenne pepper	a pinch
Fresh chives, minced	1 tablespoon

This classic dish is always hip and gets a laugh! There are lots of ways to make these snazzy and new again. I like deviled eggs hot and spicy, as if they got delivered from Hades just moments ago.

The secret to this dish is smoked paprika, which is available from fine gourmet grocers. Insist on a high-quality imported variety—you'll taste the difference. For a lovely presentation every time, use a pastry bag fitted with a star tip to pipe in the filling!

1. Slice the peeled eggs in half lengthwise and pinch out the yolks into a medium bowl. Set the whites aside.

2. Mash the yolks with the mayonnaise, Dijon, vinegar, hot sauce, ground mustard, salt, pepper, paprika, and cayenne, and whisk to blend until smooth.

3. Fill a piping bag fitted with an open star decorating tip and pipe the filling into the egg-white halves.

4. Garnish with chopped chives, a dusting of smoked paprika, and a sprinkle of sea salt. Refrigerate until needed or serve immediately.

OMELETS

Well-made omelets are beautiful creations, but they can be a bit intimidating. When you're holding the skillet handle and it's the moment of truth, going airborne isn't recommended. I think of omelets as a well-dressed scrambled egg. They're very basic, but carry themselves with true elegance.

I LIKE USING STAINLESS-STEEL surfaces, but the surest way to flip an omelet is to use a nonstick skillet and plenty of oil or butter.

ADD ABOUT A TEASPOON of water to the eggs and whisk in a large bowl that allows plenty of room to incorporate air into the eggs.

PRECOOK ANY VEGETABLE FILLINGS and keep them warm until you're ready to add them to the omelet.

IF FLIPPING the omelet is intimidating, place the filling on half of the egg once it's fully set, and gently fold the other half over. Slip a spatula between the skillet and the bottom of the omelet to protect the eggs from burning or drying out while the radiant heat warms the filling and melts the cheese.

BASIC CHEESE OMELET

SERVES 1

Just about any cheese works for omelets. My favorites include smoked Gouda, chèvre, or any aged, sharp cheddar. When it comes to cheese and omelets, I find that less is more. Too much and it oozes from the center and can easily burn.

Eggs	2
Milk	2 tablespoons
Unsalted butter or olive oil	2 tablespoons
Sea salt	2 pinches
Cheese (your choice), shredded or crumbled	3 ounces (¼ cup)

1. Heat a medium (7-inch) skillet over medium heat.

2. Crack the eggs into a bowl and add the milk. Whisk briskly until the eggs begin to froth. Set aside.

3. Add the butter or oil to thoroughly coat the surface of the pan. The butter should melt quickly but do not let it brown. If using oil, do not let it smoke.

4. Lightly sprinkle 1 pinch of salt into the pan.

5. Add the eggs to the center of the pan and lightly rock the pan to spread the eggs around. The eggs should sizzle upon contact. Cook for approximately 30 seconds to allow the eggs to set.

6. Gently lift one edge of the eggs and tilt the pan to allow any uncooked eggs pooling on top to run to the bottom and cook on the underside. This creates a firmer disc to flip.

7. Gently loosen the eggs from the edges of the pan with a spatula and carefully turn over with a spatula. Sprinkle the omelet with another pinch of salt and add the cheese to one half of the disc. Turn off the heat.

8. Fold the other half over to rest on top of the cheese and then slide the spatula between the pan surface and the eggs to lift the omelet away from the heat. Let the radiant heat melt the cheese as the omelet rests on the spatula in the pan. Serve within 1 minute.

FLIPPING WITHOUT FEAR

- Be sure the pan has plenty of oil or butter before you add the eggs.

- After the egg is set, carefully release the edges with a spatula and gently shake the pan to release the bottom of the omelet.

- Quickly give a forward shake to slide the omelet against the front edge and hold the pan underneath it to catch the omelet as it flips over.

Avocado and Bacon Omelet
with Home Fries (page 180)

AVOCADO AND BACON OMELET

This is a delicious combination of tastes and textures, with creamy avocado punctuated by crispy bacon. I like a sharp cheddar here. A little bit of chopped vine-ripened tomatoes, with the watery seeds removed, is a perfect addition, too.

Bacon	2 strips
Avocado	½
Unsalted butter or olive oil	2 tablespoons
Kosher salt	1 pinch
Vine-ripened tomatoes, seeded and chopped	½ cup
Basic Cheese Omelet (page 65)	1

1. Cook the bacon until it's crispy. Cool and crumble it. Set aside.

2. Scoop the flesh out of the avocado skin and cut it into ½-inch pieces. Set aside.

3. Prepare the Basic Cheese Omelet (page 65) as directed, but add the bacon, avocado, and tomatoes in Step 7 along with the sharp cheddar cheese.

AVOCADO: A NEW BREAKFAST FRUIT

Lush and buttery, avocado is a great addition to the breakfast plate, whether stuffed in an omelet or sliced and served on the side. There are a number of different varieties, but the most common is the Hass, with black-green, pebbled skin. To tell if an avocado is ripe, squeeze it gently—it should be soft to the touch, but not too soft. The easiest way to ripen an avocado is to place it in a paper bag with another piece of fruit and leave it on the counter for a day or two. Once ripe, it will keep well in the refrigerator.

To use an avocado, run a heavy knife (like a chef's knife) all the way around vertically, using the pit as your guide. Grab both halves and give them a slight twist to separate. To remove the pit, carefully but firmly whack your knife into the pit—just enough so that it holds firm. Then twist to remove the pit and scrape the pit against a bowl to remove it from the knife to avoid cutting your hand. Scoop the flesh from the skin with a spoon. Use immediately.

'SHROOMS AND SHALLOTS OMELET

Unsalted butter or olive oil	2 tablespoons
Kosher salt	1 pinch
Button or cremini mushrooms, thinly sliced	1 cup
Shallot, thinly sliced	1
Basic Cheese Omelet (page 65)	1

Mushrooms taste great in omelets but have a high water content, so sauté them ahead of time and drain them well of any cooking liquid. You'll keep the texture of the final dish light and dry. I like a good goat Gouda to pair with mushrooms.

1. Heat a medium (7-inch) skillet over medium heat. Add the butter or oil and salt.

2. Sauté the mushrooms and shallot over medium heat until softened and fragrant. Set aside in a small bowl. Wipe the skillet clean with a paper towel.

3. Prepare the Basic Cheese Omelet (page 65) as directed, but add the mushroom and shallot mixture in Step 7, along with the Gouda.

FRITTATAS
AND BREAKFAST LASAGNAS

A frittata is a cornucopia of wonderful flavors and seasoned ingredients baked in an egg casserole. I like bringing them to the brunch table when guests are already gathered for a dramatic presentation. Frittatas can include just about anything you want—cheese, meats, or vegetables—with potatoes providing a lot of the substance. A strata is just like a frittata but is made with stale bread instead of potatoes. Sometimes I even do a combination of bread and potatoes! If you want to go all bread, just substitute it for the amount of potatoes specified in the recipe. Breakfast lasagna involves the same type of ingredients; they're just organized differently and the starch comes in the form of noodles.

ALWAYS PRECOOK your potatoes and other vegetables before adding them to the frittata.

POTATOES ARE ESPECIALLY TENDER when cooked, so gently fold them into the egg batter during the final assembly. If all of the pieces retain their natural shape, the final product will look more elegant.

FOR A SPECIAL TOUCH, I like to crack a few eggs onto the top of the assembled frittata just before it goes into the oven.

BAKE AT 300°F TO 325°F and use a heavy-duty casserole dish. This will help prevent scorching the eggs at the edges of the pan.

POTATO-'SHROOM FRITTATA

Large Yukon Gold potatoes	2 cups
Yellow onion	½ cup
Assorted fresh mushrooms, thinly sliced	5 ounces (about 2 cups)
Olive oil	1 tablespoon, plus extra for the dish
Kosher salt	as needed
Freshly ground black pepper	as needed
Dried, ground rosemary	1 teaspoon
Eggs	10 to 12
Smoked Gouda, shredded	5 ounces (about 1 cup)
Scallions, sliced	¼ cup
Dried chervil	1 teaspoon
Sea salt	as needed
Paprika	¼ teaspoon

This debuted at Love Café and was immediately a hit! I stumbled on a great combination of ingredients after tinkering with different recipes for a while. The secret is the cheese—smoked Gouda really adds robust flavor.

1. Preheat the oven to 375°F and place a rack in the middle.

2. Peel and slice the potatoes and onion thinly by hand, with a mandoline, or in a food processor using the slicer attachment.

3. In a large bowl, combine the potato mixture with the mushrooms, oil, 1 teaspoon each of the kosher salt and pepper, and the rosemary and toss well with a flexible spatula. Spread it on a baking sheet lined with parchment paper and roast uncovered for 30 minutes, until the potatoes are soft when poked with a fork.

4. Coat the bottom and sides of a deep 9-by-13-inch casserole dish with oil and lightly sprinkle with kosher salt. Set aside.

5. Crack the eggs into a large bowl, add 2 teaspoons water, and whip by hand with a balloon whisk for 1 minute to add air.

6. Using the flexible spatula, gently combine the cheese, scallions, chervil, 1 teaspoon each of the sea salt and the pepper, and the paprika with 10 eggs, then fold in the roasted vegetables.

7. Pour everything into the oiled casserole dish. For a special touch, crack 2 more eggs on the top of the frittata and sprinkle with sea salt and pepper.

8. Reduce the temperature to 325°F and bake, uncovered, for 45 to 50 minutes, until the edges brown and the center doesn't jiggle or appear wet. Test with a meat thermometer—the internal temperature should read 160°F.

9. Remove the frittata from the oven and allow to rest for about 10 minutes before serving. Leftovers reheat well if warmed in the microwave for 20 to 25 seconds.

LOW-COUNTRY FRITTATA

White potatoes	4 to 5 medium
Yams (or sweet potatoes, if available)	3 to 4 medium
Fresh rosemary	leaves from 2 sprigs
Fresh sage, minced	about 6 broad leaves
Unsalted butter, melted	5 tablespoons
Olive oil	1 teaspoon, plus extra for the dish
Sea salt	1½ teaspoons
Sausage links	2
Yellow onions, thinly sliced	3
Celery stalks, sliced	3
Fresh cremini mushrooms, sliced	4 ounces (about 1½ cups)
Eggs	10
Fresh medium shrimp	8 ounces, peeled and deveined, tails removed
Chèvre	3 to 4 ounces, crumbled
Paprika	a pinch
Cumin seeds	a pinch
Freshly ground black pepper	a pinch

Frittatas are great for combining lots of different flavors and, in this version, I've borrowed a little bit from the Creole traditions of New Orleans and the African influence of the Carolina Low Country. This is a hearty centerpiece to any brunch.

1. Preheat the oven to 375°F and place a rack in the middle.

2. Peel and dice the potatoes and yams into ¼-inch cubes; briefly soak them in water to remove the excess starch, and drain thoroughly. Toss the cubes with the rosemary, sage, 3 tablespoons of the butter, oil, and 1 teaspoon of the salt. Spread the mixture on a baking sheet lined with parchment paper and roast, uncovered, until tender, about 35 minutes. Remove from the oven and set aside.

3. While the potatoes are roasting, roast the sausage links in the oven in a separate dish for 20 minutes. Remove and slice into ½-inch pieces.

4. In a large skillet, place the remaining 2 tablespoons butter over low heat. Add the onions, cover, and cook until thoroughly softened. Add the celery and 'shrooms and raise to medium heat. Continue to cook, covered, for another 10 minutes, or until soft to the fork. Remove from the heat and set aside.

5. Crack the eggs into a large bowl, add 2 tablespoons water, and whisk with a balloon whisk until lightly foamy. Fold the shrimp and chèvre into the eggs, followed by the potatoes, vegetables, and sausage.

6. Coat the bottom and sides of a deep 9-by-13-inch casserole dish with oil and lightly sprinkle with the remaining salt.

Pour in the frittata mixture and sprinkle the top with the paprika, cumin seeds, and pepper.

7. Reduce the temperature to 325°F and bake, uncovered, for about 50 minutes, until the edges brown and the center doesn't jiggle or appear wet. Test with a meat thermometer—the internal temperature should read 160°F.

8. Remove the frittata from the oven and allow to rest for about 10 minutes before serving. Leftovers reheat well if warmed in the microwave for 20 to 25 seconds.

BUTTERNUT SQUASH FRITTATA

Butternut squash is one of my favorite foods. I love it for the flavor, color, and numerous ways it can be served. This dish looks quite dramatic with the bright orange slices of squash, so for the sake of easy prep and the best appearance, I use only the neck, which slices into perfect rounds.

1. Preheat the oven to 375°F and place a rack in the middle.

2. Peel the squash (see Sidebar page 76) and onion and slice, along with the mushrooms, very thinly by hand with a mandoline or in a food processor fitted with the slicing attachment.

3. Place the squash and onion in a large bowl, add the mushrooms, oil, ¾ teaspoon each of the kosher salt and the pepper, and the nutmeg and toss with a flexible spatula. Spread the vegetables on a baking sheet lined with parchment paper and roast uncovered for 30 minutes, until soft to the fork.

4. Coat the bottom and sides of a deep 9-by-13-inch casserole dish with oil and lightly sprinkle with kosher salt. Set aside.

5. Crack 10 of the eggs into a large bowl, add 2 tablespoons water, and whisk for 1 minute.

6. Using a flexible spatula, gently fold in the cheeses, scallions, ½ teaspoon each of the sea salt and the pepper, the paprika, and dill, followed by the roasted vegetables.

7. Pour the frittata mixture into the prepared casserole. For a special touch, crack 3 more eggs on the top of the frittata and sprinkle with sea salt and pepper.

Butternut squash	1 pound
Yellow onion	½ cup
Fresh cremini mushrooms	5 ounces
Olive oil	2 tablespoons, plus extra for the dish
Kosher salt	¾ teaspoon
Freshly ground black pepper	as needed
Freshly grated nutmeg	½ teaspoon
Eggs	10 to 13
Smoked Gouda, shredded	3 ounces (about 1 cup)
Sharp cheddar, shredded	3 ounces (about 1 cup)
Scallions, chopped	2 tablespoons
Sea salt	as needed
Paprika	a pinch
Dried dill	a pinch

8. Reduce the temperature to 325°F and bake, uncovered, for 45 to 50 minutes, until the edges brown, and the center doesn't jiggle or appear wet. Test with a meat thermometer—the internal temperature should read 160°F.

9. Remove the frittata from the oven and allow to rest for about 10 minutes before serving. Leftovers reheat well if warmed in the microwave for 20 to 25 seconds.

A whole butternut squash can be a formidable opponent, but once you know how, it's easy to break one down—and much less expensive to buy than one that's precut by the supermarket. Using a heavy knife, cut the neck from the more bulbous bottom. Remove the stem end and then slice the neck in half or quarters before peeling and slicing. Cut the bottom in half, use a spoon to remove all the seeds, then cut it into quarters before peeling and slicing.

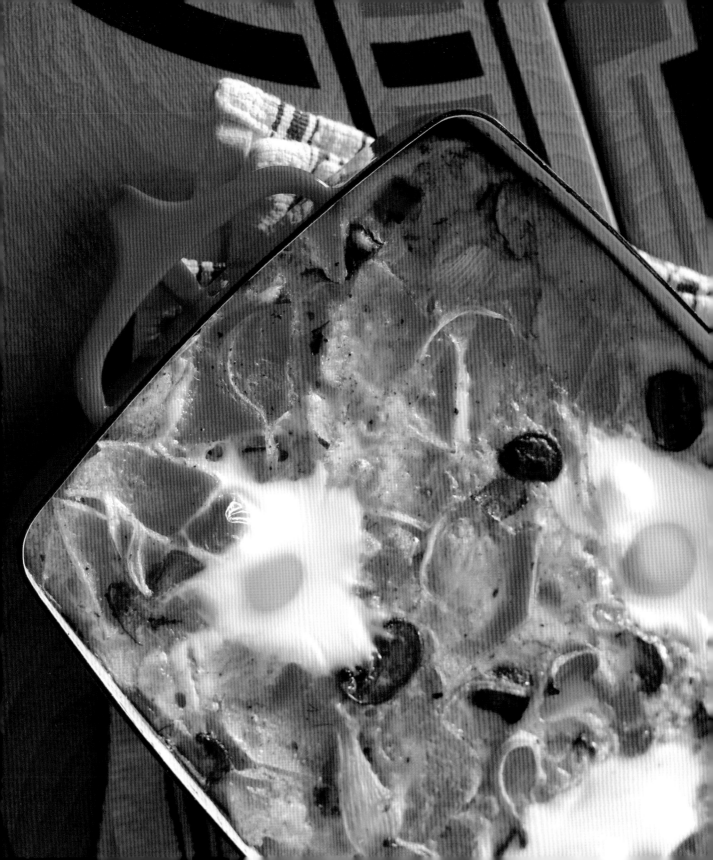

DAIRY-FREE BUTTERNUT SQUASH FRITTATA

Butternut squash	1 pound
Small white potatoes	2
Small red potato	1
Chicken stock	¼ cup, plus 2 tablespoons
Olive oil	2 tablespoons
Balsamic vinegar	2 tablespoons
Sea salt	as needed
Paprika	1 teaspoon
Cumin seeds, very finely ground	1 teaspoon
Canola oil	1 tablespoon, plus extra for the dish
Fresh cremini mushrooms, thinly sliced	3
Yellow onion, thinly sliced	½
Garlic clove, sliced	1
Liquid smoke (see Note)	1 teaspoon
Ground white pepper	to taste
Eggs	6
Scallions, finely sliced	2

No cheese, no butter, no problem! Roasting the vegetables gives them great, sweet caramelization, and good-quality chicken stock boosts the flavor quotient, too. I promise you won't miss the cheese! Another ingredient I rely on to bring in a lot of flavor is Liquid Smoke. Sounds odd, but I love it. Colgin Liquid Smoke from Texas should be readily available at grocery stores and is always available online.

1. Preheat the oven to 375°F and set the rack on the middle shelf.

2. Peel the squash (see Sidebar page 76) and dice it, along with the potatoes, into ¼-inch cubes.

3. In a large bowl, toss to combine the squash, potatoes, ¼ cup of the stock, olive oil, vinegar, 1 tablespoon salt, paprika, and cumin. Spread on a baking sheet lined with parchment and sprinkle with more salt if you like. Roast, uncovered, for 40 minutes, or until the vegetables are tender and browned. Remove from the oven and set aside.

4. Meanwhile, pour the canola oil into a large skillet over high heat. Add the mushrooms, onion, garlic, liquid smoke, ½ teaspoon salt, and pepper, and sauté until softened. Set aside.

5. Coat the bottom and sides of a deep 9-by-13-inch casserole dish with oil and lightly sprinkle with salt. Set aside.

6. Crack the eggs into a large bowl and add 1 tablespoon water and the remaining 2 tablespoons stock. Whip with a balloon whisk for 1 minute to add air.

7. Using a flexible spatula, fold in the scallions, followed by the sautéed vegetables, and then the roasted vegetables.

8. Pour the frittata mixture into the oiled casserole and lightly season to taste with sea salt.

9. Reduce the temperature to 325°F and bake for approximately 50 minutes, until the edges brown and the center doesn't jiggle or appear wet. Test with a meat thermometer—the internal temperature should read 160°F.

10. Remove the frittata from the oven and allow to rest for about 10 minutes before serving. Leftovers reheat well if warmed in the microwave for 20 to 25 seconds.

NOTE:
Liquid smoke is made from capturing and condensing the vapors from burning wood chips. A few drops bring a smoky goodness to all kinds of dishes—it's a great way to boost flavor without adding meat or extra salt.

BREAKFAST LASAGNA

Unsalted butter	2 ounces (½ stick)
Unbleached all-purpose flour	2 tablespoons
Sea salt	as needed
Milk, warm	3 cups
Freshly ground black pepper	as needed
Vegetable oil	3 tablespoons
Fresh mushrooms (cremini, button, shiitake), thinly sliced	2 pounds
Yellow onion, thinly sliced	1
Applewood smoked bacon	1 pound
Eggs	9
No-boil lasagna noodles	9
Smoked Gouda, shredded	6 ounces (about 2 cups)
Sharp cheddar cheese, shredded	6 ounces (about 2 cups)
Paprika	a pinch

One of the best parts about breakfast and brunch is the casual nature of it all. Pretty much anything goes if it tastes good. This dish gets raised eyebrows all of the time. All the ingredients come together to create a delicious main course. It's a really big dish that doesn't disappoint. The recipe can be doubled if you have an extra-deep pan.

1. Melt 2 tablespoons of the butter in a medium saucepan. Stir in the flour and ¼ teaspoon salt and cook until it reaches a light blond color.

2. Slowly whisk in the milk and continue stirring until it lightly simmers. Add ¼ teaspoon pepper. Remove from the heat, cover with a lid, and set aside.

3. Preheat the oven to 350°F. Coat the bottom of a 9-by-13-inch baking dish with butter, then sprinkle lightly with salt and black pepper.

4. In a deep skillet, heat the vegetable oil over medium heat. Add the salt, and sauté the 'shrooms and onion until they are cooked down to about half the volume, approximately 5 minutes.

5. Cook the bacon in the microwave until crispy. Set aside to cool and then crumble it.

6. Crack 6 of the eggs into a large bowl and whisk to scramble.

7. Melt the remaining butter in a large nonstick pan and add the beaten eggs. Cook them about halfway—leaving them very loose and wet.

8. Using a ladle, spread a thin coating of the béchamel sauce on the bottom of the prepared pan and cover with 3 lasagna noodles.

9. Spread more sauce on top of the noodles, then layer half of the 'shrooms and onions, followed by half of the Gouda.

10. Add another layer of 3 lasagna noodles, then spread with the partially cooked scrambled eggs, half of the cheddar cheese, and more of the sauce.

11. Add the final layer of 3 lasagna noodles. Cover with the remaining sauce, 'shrooms and onions, and the remaining cheeses. Sprinkle salt, pepper, and paprika across the top.

12. Create 3 tablespoon-size wells in the top layer, then crack and drop one of the remaining eggs into each one.

13. Bake for 30 to 40 minutes, or until the sides bubble and the top is lightly browned. Place a baking sheet on the shelf above if the cheese is browning.

14. Remove from the oven and let the lasagna rest for 10 to 15 minutes before slicing it into squares to serve.

SALSA LASAGNA

Olive oil	2 tablespoons
Sea salt	to taste
Garlic cloves, thinly sliced	5 to 6
Green peppers, thinly sliced	2
Eggs	12
Unsalted butter	2 tablespoons
Tomato salsa	1 to 2 (16-ounce) jars
No-boil lasagna noodles	9
Black beans	1 (12- to 16-ounce) can
Red onion, very thinly sliced	¾ cup
Monterey jack cheese, freshly grated	6 ounces (about 2 cups)
Sharp cheddar cheese, freshly grated	6 ounces (about 2 cups)
Cilantro, leaves only, torn	½ cup
Frozen corn kernels	1½ cup
Freshly ground black pepper	to taste
Paprika	to taste
Avocados, sliced	2

Even though I love to cook, I try to keep things simple on the weekends. Go ahead and use jarred sauce to make life easier. No matter what you use, this lasagna is bound to taste good coming out of the oven, piping hot and oozing melted cheese!

1. Preheat the oven to 350°F. Coat the bottom of a 9-by-13-inch baking dish with butter, then sprinkle lightly with salt and pepper.

2. In a medium skillet, heat the olive oil and a pinch of salt over medium heat. Add the garlic and green peppers and lightly sauté to soften. Set aside.

3. Crack the eggs into a large bowl and whisk to scramble.

4. Melt the butter in a large nonstick pan over low to medium heat and add the beaten eggs. Cook them about halfway, leaving them very loose and wet.

5. Spread a layer of salsa on the bottom of the prepared baking dish and cover it with 3 lasagna noodles.

6. Spread more salsa on top of the noodles, then a layer of half of the black beans, red onion, and sautéed green peppers and garlic, followed by half of the Monterey jack and cheddar cheeses.

7. Add another layer of 3 lasagna noodles, then spread out the partially cooked scrambled eggs, cilantro, and remaining cheddar cheese.

8. Add the final layer of 3 noodles. Cover with the remaining salsa, beans, onions, garlic and green pepper, Monterey jack cheese, and the corn. Sprinkle with salt, pepper, and paprika to taste, then arrange the avocado slices decoratively across the top.

9. Bake for 30 to 40 minutes, or until the sides bubble and the top is lightly browned. Loosely cover with aluminum foil if the top is cooking too fast.

10. Remove from the oven and let the lasagna rest for 10 to 15 minutes before slicing it into squares to serve.

KEEP ALL OF YOUR INGREDIENTS *COLD*.

I ADD A LITTLE SUGAR to my dough. It helps to tenderize it and round out the flavor.

ACCURATELY MEASURE all of your ingredients.

QUICHE

Aside from being the quintessential dish for brunch, a quiche is ideal for any gathering since it's very easy to reheat if made a day or two ahead of time. Quiches travel well, too, for a potluck or picnic. Store the quiche in the same dish in which it was baked and reheat in a cold oven at 275°F until warmed through, or place it on a plate and nuke at thirty-second intervals until hot.

Once you get the crust down, a world of options opens up. You can fill a quiche with just about anything you want and the combo will generally taste good—because it's wrapped in flour and butter!

USE SEA SALT instead of generic table salt. The difference in flavor really comes through.

QUICKLY CUT small pieces of cold butter into the flour, and slowly add cold liquid to bring it all together.

HANDLE THE DOUGH GENTLY and touch it as little as possible.

WHITE FLOUR CRUST

This recipe yields enough dough for two 9-inch pans, the common size for ovenproof glass bakeware. Wrap any leftover dough tightly in plastic wrap and store it in the fridge for up to 1 week or the freezer for up to 1 month. You can also roll out the extra dough, cut it out with seasonal cookie cutters, and bake great decorations for the serving plate.

Unsalted butter	5 ounces (1¼ stick)
Unbleached all-purpose flour	10 ounces (2 cups)
Sea salt	1 teaspoon
Superfine sugar	1 tablespoon (optional)
Ice-cold vodka (unflavored)	2 tablespoons (optional)
Egg	1
Vanilla extract	1 splash (¼ teaspoon or less)

1. Cut the butter into small pieces and refrigerate or freeze to make them very cold.

2. Preheat the oven to 400°F and set the rack in the middle.

3. Sift the flour with the salt and sugar, if using, into a large bowl. In a cup, combine the vodka with 3 tablespoons ice water (or use 5 tablespoons ice water and no vodka, if you prefer).

4. Rub or cut the butter into the flour with your fingers to make a crumbly meal.

5. Slowly add the ice water (and vodka, if using) while turning the mixture with a fork. The dough will form a ball and come off the sides of the bowl when it's ready. You can also make the dough in a food processor, pulsing the butter and flour to a crumbly meal, and then slowing adding the ice water while pulsing until the dough forms a ball.

6. Remove the dough ball from the bowl, divide it in half, and lightly pat each ball with flour. If you're only making one crust, wrap the second dough ball in plastic and refrigerate or freeze for later use.

7. Place the dough you are using between sheets of parchment paper and roll out to a 10- to 11-inch disc. Remove one sheet of paper, lay the dough over a pie pan, and peel

I use a mixture of ice-cold water and vodka for my dough. The alcohol doesn't activate the gluten proteins in the flour, but does help the dough come together, leaving the crust flaky and light.

Pie Dough

Pie Dough
- process

Pie Dough
- process
- Rest
- Roll out

Pie Dough
- process
- Rest
- Roll out
- Trim + Fold

off the remaining paper. Ease the dough into the pan; cut the excess and crimp the edges. Refrigerate for at least 5 minutes.

8. In a small bowl, whisk together the egg and vanilla extract. With a pastry brush, lightly coat the sides and crimped edge of the crust with the egg wash to enhance the color.

9. Prick the bottom of the crust with a fork, line it with parchment paper, and place dry beans or pie weights in the center all the way to the sides. Blind bake the crust for 10 minutes (see Sidebar). Let the crust cool completely on a wire rack, then remove the parchment and weights.

WHOLE-WHEAT FLOUR CRUST

This crust yields an earthy flavor and tender bite. The touch of cornmeal gives it a toasty crunch that helps brighten the flavor. Use the same preparation method as the White Flour Crust. Because the whole-wheat crust tends to be more crumbly, a bit of egg is added for binding in lieu of cold water. Not all of the egg will be necessary; use what's left over for the wash to give the crust more color.

Unsalted butter, softened **4 ounces (1 stick)**

Whole-wheat flour **6 ounces (1½ cups)**

Superfine sugar **1 tablespoon**

Cornmeal **1½ teaspoons**

Salt **½ teaspoon**

Ice-cold vodka (unflavored) **2 tablespoons (optional)**

Egg **1**

Vanilla extract **1 splash (¼ teaspoon or less)**

1. Prepare the dough as for the White Flour Crust (page 85), incorporating 2 to 3 tablespoons beaten egg along with the water in step 5.

BLIND BAKING

It's important to prebake the crust for a quiche so the bottom of your finished product won't be soggy. Follow these steps to prevent the bottom from puffing up and over the sides of the pan: Prick the bottom of the unbaked crust with a fork (this is called *docking*) then line the crust with parchment paper and place dry beans or baking weights on top to prevent the dough from puffing up. Bake in a preheated oven as specified.

ROASTED TOMATOES

Roma tomatoes	3 pounds
Olive oil	½ cup
Balsamic vinegar	¼ cup
Kosher salt	3 tablespoons
Black pepper	to taste
Garlic	5 cloves, minced or pressed
Yellow onion, thinly sliced	1
Fresh rosemary, chopped	1 tablespoon
Fresh sage, chopped	1 tablespoon

During the harvest season, I'll buy tomatoes by the bucketful for slow roasting and canning. I try to keep roasted tomatoes on hand for everyday use. They're a delicious addition and make the average dish exciting.

1. Preheat the oven to 225°F and place a rack in the middle.

2. Core the tomatoes and squeeze them over a bowl to release their seeds and juice. Cut them into quarters.

3. Toss the tomatoes in a bowl with the remaining ingredients.

4. Place the mixture on a baking sheet lined with parchment paper. Place the sheet in the oven and bake for 4 to 5 hours.

5. Store the tomatoes in an airtight container for up to 2 weeks or submerged in olive oil in the refrigerator for up to 2 months.

ROASTED TOMATO QUICHE WITH BACON AND ANDOUILLE SAUSAGE

This is a bit more like a meat-lover's breakfast pie than a light and delicate quiche. It's great for those times when you want to indulge in heartier fare. Roasted garlic adds an extra richness.

1. Preheat the oven to 350°F and place a rack in the middle.

2. Prepare the pie crust as directed and set aside.

3. Cook the bacon until crisp. Set aside to cool, then chop it into bite-size pieces.

4. Cook the sausage and cut it into slices.

5. Crack the eggs into a large bowl and whisk to blend. Stir in the half-and-half, garlic, anise seeds, and nutmeg.

6. Spread the tomatoes, meats, and half of the cheeses across the bottom of the crust, then pour the egg mixture over. Top with the remaining cheese and sprinkle with salt and pepper.

7. Bake for 50 minutes or until the center is set, edges bubble, and the quiche appears golden across the top. Remove it to a wire rack to rest for 10 minutes before serving.

White Flour Crust (page 85) or Whole-Wheat Flour Crust (page 87), blind baked and cooled	1
Thick-cut bacon	6 strips
Andouille sausage	1 link
Eggs	6
Half-and-half	½ cup
Roasted garlic	2 tablespoons
Anise seeds	½ teaspoon, crushed
Nutmeg, freshly grated	½ teaspoon
Roasted Tomatoes (page 88)	1½ cups
Gouda, shredded	4½ ounces (1½ cups)
Parmesan, grated	2 ounces (½ cup)
Kosher salt	1 teaspoon
Freshly ground black pepper	1 teaspoon

QUICHE FLORENTINE

White Flour Crust (page 85) or Whole-Wheat Flour Crust (page 87), blind baked and cooled	1
Olive oil	2 tablespoons
Shallots, thinly sliced	¼ cup
Baby spinach	1½ cups
Thick-cut bacon	4 to 5 strips
Eggs	8
Ricotta cheese	1 cup
Freshly grated nutmeg	½ teaspoon
Milk	up to ½ cup
Parmesan cheese, grated	3 ounces (¾ cup)
Sea salt	¼ to ½ teaspoon
Freshly ground black pepper	¼ to ½ teaspoon

Otherwise known as spinach quiche, this classic quiche holds the top spot for good reason. It's delicious! You can swap frozen spinach for fresh; just be sure to squeeze out absolutely all of the water.

1. Preheat the oven to 350°F and place a rack in the middle.

2. Prepare the pie crust as directed and set aside.

3. Heat the oil in a small skillet over high heat. Add the shallots and sauté until soft. Set aside to cool.

4. Wash, dry, and roughly chop the spinach.

5. Cook the bacon until crisp. Set aside to cool, then chop it into bite-size pieces.

6. Crack the eggs into a large bowl and whisk to blend. Fold in the cooked shallots, ricotta cheese, and nutmeg. Add the milk as necessary to loosen the mixture so that it is loose but not runny in the bowl.

7. Spread the spinach, bacon, and Parmesan on the bottom of the crust, then pour the egg mixture over. Sprinkle with salt and pepper.

8. Bake for 30 to 35 minutes, or until the center is set, the edges bubble, and the quiche appears golden across the top. Remove it to a wire rack to rest for 10 minutes before serving.

RED AND YELLOW PEPPER QUICHE

Roasted peppers make a splash of color that's inviting and just slightly sweet. Charring fresh peppers is very gourmet, but canned ones work perfectly well, too. Just drain and pat them dry before using.

1. Preheat the oven to 350°F and place a rack in the middle.

2. Prepare the pie crust as directed and set aside.

3. Cook the bacon until crisp. Set aside to cool, then chop it into bite-size pieces.

4. Crack the eggs into a large bowl and whisk to blend. Stir in the garlic powder and half-and-half.

5. Spread the pepper strips and cheeses across the bottom of the crust and pour the egg mixture over. Sprinkle with salt and pepper.

6. Bake for 45 to 50 minutes, or until the center is set, the edges bubble, and the quiche appears golden across the top. Remove it to a wire rack to rest for 10 minutes before serving.

White Flour Crust (page 85) or Whole-Wheat Flour Crust (page 87), blind baked and cooled	1
Bacon	4 strips
Eggs	8
Garlic powder	½ teaspoon
Half-and-half	½ cup
Red bell peppers, roasted and cut into ½-inch strips	2
Yellow bell peppers, roasted and cut into ½-inch strips	2
Fontina cheese, shredded	3 to 4 ounces (1½ cups)
Buffalo mozzarella, sliced	4 ounces (1 cup)
Salt	¼ teaspoon
Freshly ground black pepper	¼ teaspoon

To roast fresh peppers, char them whole over an open flame until blackened. Place the charred peppers into a paper bag and fold down to let them steam. Once the peppers have cooled, remove the stem, cut them in half, and remove the pith and all of the seeds. Cut the peppers into quarters and use a sharp knife to peel away all of the charred skin before slicing into ½-inch strips.

MUFFINS, SCONES, AND BISCUITS

Here are breakfast treats that can be eaten out of hand. A basket of muffins, or a platter of scones and biscuits, won't be around for long. Delicious on their own or slathered with butter and jam, this is lovin' straight from the oven!

LIGHTLY SPRAY THE MUFFIN PAN with nonstick spray before inserting the paper liners. The paper may get a bit greasy, but the risk of losing the muffin caps really goes down.

DEFINITELY UNDERMIX THE BATTER; you want to see patches of flour. If using a mixer, scoop in half of the flour mixture and mix, but then gently fold in the rest by hand.

MUFFINS

Muffins are the quintessential morning treat. You can bake them in batches, wrap them tightly, and freeze. Or prep the ingredients at night and toss 'em together in the morning. They'll bake in no time and you've got a homemade breakfast plus a few to spare. Sugar, butter, eggs, nuts, and more find a happy harmony in simple combinations that showcase a tender texture and crunchy muffin cap. And speaking of that muffin cap, if you enjoy channeling Elaine from *Seinfeld* and the top is your favorite part of the muffin, invest in a muffin cap pan with suitably shallow baking wells.

SPRINKLE SEVERAL PINCHES of turbinado sugar and a mix of spices on top to create the crunchy and sparkly muffin top that feels and sounds so good when you bite into it.

MUFFIN CAPS BAKE IN ABOUT HALF the time as regular muffins. Test for doneness with a skewer: It should come out clean when poked, and appear golden across the top and edges

BLUEBERRY MUFFINS

Bursting with ripe berries, served warm from the oven, split and melting sweet butter—in my mind, muffins can't get better than this! Blueberries are the classic choice, but you can easily substitute raspberries, sliced strawberries, small blackberries, or a combination of berries.

1. Preheat the oven to 350°F and place a rack in the middle.

2. In a large bowl, gently whisk to combine the flour, starch, the confectioners' and turbinado sugars, baking powder, and salt and set aside. Combine the eggs, milk, half-and-half, and vanilla in a separate bowl and set aside.

3. Toss the blueberries with 2 teaspoons of the liquid ingredients and 2 tablespoons of the flour mix in a medium bowl.

4. In a stand mixer fitted with the paddle attachment, mix the superfine sugar and butter for 2 to 3 minutes on low speed.

5. With the mixer running, slowly drizzle the liquid mixture into the butter and sugar. It will look lumpy like cottage cheese.

6. Quickly add the flour mixture in 3 scoopfuls. Mix for about 5 seconds. Do not fully combine.

7. Immediately stop the mixer and fold the berries in by hand with a rubber spatula. You will have dry patches—that's good.

8. Spray the muffin pan really well with nonstick spray, then line with paper liners.

Unbleached all-purpose flour, sifted	9 ounces (scant 2 cups)
Potato starch	1 ounce
Confectioners' sugar	2 tablespoons
Turbinado sugar	1 tablespoon, plus more for garnish
Baking powder	2 teaspoons
Sea salt	½ teaspoon
Eggs	3
Milk	¼ cup
Half-and-half	1 tablespoon
Vanilla extract	1 teaspoon
Fresh blueberries	8 ounces
Superfine sugar	6 ounces (¾ cup)
Unsalted butter, very soft	4 ounces (1 stick)

9. To get a big muffin cap, fill the liners to the top. Sprinkle the tops with a little turbinado sugar.

10. Bake for 22 to 24 minutes, or until a skewer inserted in the center of a muffin comes out clean. The muffins should be light and golden in appearance.

11. Remove from the oven and allow them to rest in the pan for at least 5 minutes before serving.

Toss small bits of fruit or nuts with a bit of flour mix and a little milk before folding them into the batter. This helps lock them in place rather than sink to the bottom during baking.

Blueberry (page 97) and
Lemon-Almond (page 100) Muffins

LEMON-ALMOND MUFFINS

FOR THE MUFFINS

Unbleached all-purpose flour	10 ounces (2 cups)
Confectioners' sugar	½ cup
Baking powder	2 teaspoons
Salt	½ teaspoon
Eggs	3
Milk	¼ cup
Heavy cream	2 tablespoons
Fresh lemon juice	1 tablespoon
Lemon zest	1 teaspoon
Vanilla extract	1 teaspoon
Unsalted butter, very soft	4 ounces (1 stick)
Superfine sugar	6 ounces (¾ cup)
Sliced almonds, roasted	½ cup

FOR THE TOPPING

Sliced almonds	½ cup
Superfine sugar	2 tablespoons
Milk	1 tablespoon
Vanilla extract	¼ teaspoon
Turbinado sugar	for garnish

Right before I entered law school I lived in Hollywood, which was quite an experience. I shared a place with my sister, and the grocer down the street baked the best lemon-almond muffins. I still dream about them, the perfect partner for my 45-minute commute to San Fernando.

1. Preheat the oven to 350°F and place a rack in the middle.

2. In a large bowl, gently whisk to combine the flour, confectioners' sugar, baking powder, and salt. Set aside. In another bowl, whisk to combine the eggs, milk, cream, lemon juice, zest, and vanilla. Set aside.

3. In a stand mixer fitted with the paddle attachment, mix the butter, superfine sugar, and almonds on low speed for 2 minutes, or 1 minute for muffin caps.

4. With the mixer running, slowly drizzle the liquid mixture into the butter and sugar. It will look lumpy like cottage cheese.

5. Quickly add the flour mixture in 3 scoopfuls. Stop the mixer and fold it a bit by hand. Do not fully combine.

6. To make the topping: In a small bowl, whisk to combine the almonds, sugar, milk, and vanilla and set aside.

7. Spray the muffin pan really well with nonstick spray, then line with paper liners.

8. To get a big muffin cap, fill the liners to the top. Drop large clumps of the almond topping onto the batter for each muffin and gently press into place. Sprinkle the tops with a little turbinado sugar.

9. Bake for 22 to 24 minutes, or until a skewer inserted in the center of a muffin comes out clean. The muffins should be light and golden in appearance.

10. Remove from the oven and allow them to rest in the pan for at least 5 minutes before serving.

I love muffins, but always prefer caps. Nothing beats the crunchy edges, and they aren't nearly as filling as a whole muffin.

MORNING GLORY MUFFINS

Unbleached all-purpose flour	5 ounces (1 cup)
Superfine sugar	½ cup
Shredded coconut, unsweetened	¼ cup
Pecans, whole	¼ cup
Baking powder	½ teaspoon
Ground cinnamon	¼ teaspoon
Sea salt	¼ teaspoon
Ground mace	pinch (optional)
Carrot, peeled and grated	¾ cup
Apple (Gala or Fuji), peeled and grated	½
Dried pineapple, finely chopped	½ cup
Rice bran, grapeseed, or canola oil	6 tablespoons
Zucchini, grated	¼ cup
Raisins or currants	¼ cup
Eggs	1½
Vanilla extract	½ teaspoon

It seems unlikely that this long and varied list of ingredients would come together and taste like cake, but it works and is one of the tastiest muffins you'll find. The first time I had one, I was blown away at this nubby mass of goodness.

1. Preheat the oven to 350°F and place a rack in the middle.

2. In a large bowl, gently whisk to combine the flour, sugar, coconut, pecans, baking powder, cinnamon, salt, and mace and set aside. Combine the carrot, apple, pineapple, oil, zucchini, raisins, eggs, and vanilla in a separate bowl and set aside.

3. Stir the liquid mixture into the flour mixture with a wooden spoon.

4. Spray the muffin pan really well with nonstick spray, then line with paper liners.

5. Scoop ¼ cup batter into each paper liner.

6. Bake for 30 minutes, or until a skewer inserted in the center of a muffin comes out clean. The muffins should be light and golden in appearance.

7. Remove from the oven and allow them to rest in the pan for at least 5 minutes before serving. Leave plain or top with Cream Cheese Drizzle (page 50) and Apple Curls (page 21).

Morning Glory Muffins with
Cream Cheese Drizzle (page 50)
and Apple Curls (page 21)

BANANA-WALNUT MUFFINS

Here's another way to enjoy the flavor of banana bread, but with a lightness that's only possible in a muffin. The paper liner provides most of the structure for this really tender cake. Don't mix the batter too hard—in fact, fold slowly and barely blend it together at all.

1. Preheat the oven to 350°F and place a rack in the middle.

2. Grind the oats to a powder in a spice grinder, then whisk to combine in a large bowl with the flour, turbinado sugar, baking powder, and salt. Set aside. Combine the bananas, eggs, yolk, cream, lemon juice, and vanilla in a separate bowl and set aside.

3. If you're adding the chocolate (and you should!), toss it together in a small bowl with 1 tablespoon of the liquid ingredients and 1 tablespoon of the flour mix. Set aside.

4. In a stand mixer fitted with the paddle attachment, mix the superfine sugar, butter, and walnuts on low speed for 2 minutes.

5. With the mixer running, slowly drizzle the liquid mixture into the butter and sugar. It will look lumpy like cottage cheese.

6. Quickly add the flour mixture in 3 scoopfuls. Mix for about 5 seconds. Stop the mixer and fold in the chocolate chunks by hand. Do not fully combine.

7. To make the topping: Whisk to combine the walnuts, syrup, and vanilla together in a bowl and set aside.

8. Spray the muffin pan really well with nonstick spray, then line with paper liners.

FOR THE MUFFINS

Whole rolled oats	1 tablespoon
Unbleached all-purpose flour	10 ounces (2 cups)
Turbinado sugar	2 tablespoons, plus extra for sprinkling
Baking powder	1 tablespoon
Salt	½ teaspoon
Bananas, very ripe, mashed well	¾ cup
Eggs	2
Egg yolk	1
Heavy cream	2 tablespoons
Fresh lemon juice	1 teaspoon
Vanilla extract	1 teaspoon
Bittersweet chocolate, cut in ¼-inch chunks	½ to ¾ cup (optional)
Superfine sugar	¾ cup
Unsalted butter, soft	4 ounces (1 stick)
Walnut pieces, roasted	½ cup

FOR THE TOPPING

Walnut pieces, roasted	½ cup
Sugar syrup (see Sidebar page 106)	1 tablespoon
Vanilla extract	¼ teaspoon

9. To get a big muffin cap, fill the papers to the top. Drop large clumps of the walnut topping onto the batter and gently press into place. Sprinkle with a little turbinado sugar.

10. Bake for 22 to 24 minutes, or until a skewer inserted in the center of a muffin comes out clean. The muffins should be light and golden in appearance.

11. Remove from the oven and allow them to rest in the pan for at least 5 minutes before serving.

SUGAR SYRUP

Sugar syrup has any number of uses, from baking to cocktail mixing to the best homemade lemonade. This is my favorite recipe; it yields a thicker syrup than a basic simple syrup. It's a little more than a two-to-one ratio of sugar to water. The extra quarter cup of water helps prevent the sugar from recrystallizing.

Combine 16 ounces (2 cups) superfine sugar and 1¼ cup water in a small saucepan. Simmer over medium heat, stirring occasionally, until the sugar is dissolved. Remove and let cool to room temperature. Transfer to a covered container for storage in the refrigerator indefinitely.

SCONES

There are a lot of nonbelievers out there who simply don't care for scones. I understand. I've tasted some awful, dry, coffee-shop versions in my day. Those are not my scones. With the right ingredients in the proper ratios, scones are delightful.

All of these recipes yield a resilient dough that can be mixed and shaped in advance and held in the fridge or freezer for several days if wrapped tightly. Bring to room temperature and coat with the egg wash immediately before baking.

WHOLE-WHEAT FLOUR doesn't absorb the liquid ingredients very well, so the dough will feel tacky and sticky.

FOR A LOWER-CALORIE SCONE, substitute skim milk or even soy milk for the heavy cream. But try the recipes as written before venturing off script so you'll know what they should taste like.

FOR A TENDER SCONE use very cold butter and don't overhandle the dough.

THE AMOUNT OF LIQUID needed to form a proper dough varies. Weather, the humidity in your kitchen, the temperature of your butter, and other factors all play a role.

I PREFER TO MIX the dough by hand, but if your arms get tired, there's no harm in using a stand mixer; just don't overmix.

THE "STARTER" SCONE

Unbleached all-purpose flour	10 ounces (2 cups)
Granulated sugar	½ cup, plus extra for sprinkling
Turbinado sugar	2 tablespoons
Baking powder	2 teaspoons
Kosher salt	½ teaspoon
Table salt	½ teaspoon
Unsalted butter, very cold	4 ounces (1 stick)
Heavy cream	up to 1 cup
Egg	1
Vanilla extract	a dash, a splash, you can't have too much
Sea salt	for sprinkling

Scones are a great blank canvas and I often use this recipe as a base when I want to experiment with new flavors. If you're new to scones, try this recipe a few times to get a feel for how the dough comes together. Then you can give it your own spin by adding up to ½ cup of dried fruit or nuts, or 1 to 2 teaspoons of freshly cut herbs. Notice that the recipes call for different salts, too. It's best to use a variety of salts in order to create a balance of complex flavors. Just watch out for any large crystals; crush them before adding to the dough.

1. Preheat the oven to 375°F and place a rack in the middle. Line a baking sheet with parchment paper or a silicone baking mat.

2. In a large bowl, combine the flour, sugars, baking powder, and salts. Whisk for about 10 seconds and set aside.

3. Cut the butter into small pieces, then cut the pieces into the flour mixture using your fingers, a fork, or a stand mixer fitted with the paddle attachment set on low speed. Once the flour and butter clump together when pinched, slowly add the cream a little at a time while turning the dough. Stop when the dough easily forms a ball—it may not be necessary to use all of the cream.

4. The dough should feel light and barely moist. Place a handful of it on a lightly floured surfaced to shape into a 4-inch square that's about ¾ inch thick.

5. Cut the square from corner to corner twice to make four triangles. Repeat with the remaining dough to make as many scones as the dough provides.

6. Mix the egg and vanilla together in a small bowl. Either quickly dunk each scone in the wash or use a pastry brush to dab the top and sides.

7. Place the scones on the prepared baking sheet and sprinkle the tops with granulated sugar and a tiny pinch of sea salt.

8. Bake for about 15 minutes, or until the scones are lightly browned on the sides and golden across the top. Cool on racks for 5 minutes before serving.

OATMEAL-RAISIN SCONES

Heavy cream, whole milk, or soy milk	¼ cup
Maple syrup	¼ teaspoon
Unbleached all-purpose flour	8 ounces (1½ cups)
Raisins	½ cup
Whole rolled oats	2 ounces (¼ cup)
Turbinado or maple sugar	3 tablespoons, plus extra for sprinkling
Cornmeal	1 tablespoon
Cream of tartar	1½ teaspoons
Baking soda	¾ teaspoon
Sea salt	½ teaspoon, plus extra for sprinkling
Unsalted butter, very cold	4 ounces (1 stick)
Egg	1
Vanilla extract	½ teaspoon

Oatmeal and raisins make a fabulous combination in scones, and it's even better with a little maple sugar substituted for the turbinado. You can find maple sugar in the specialty foods section of your gourmet grocer. The first bite always reminds me of a bowl of hot cereal on a winter day. You can substitute currants for the raisins here as well.

1. Preheat the oven to 375°F and place a rack in the middle. Line a baking sheet with parchment paper or a silicone baking mat.

2. In a small bowl, stir together the cream and syrup and set aside.

3. In a large bowl, combine the flour, raisins, oats, sugar, cornmeal, cream of tartar, baking soda, and salt. Whisk for about 10 seconds and set aside.

4. Cut the butter into small pieces, then cut the pieces into the flour mixture using your fingers, a fork, or a stand mixer fitted with the paddle attachment set on low speed. Once the flour and butter clump together when pinched, slowly add the cream mixture a little at a time while turning the dough. Stop when the dough easily forms a ball—it may not be necessary to use all of the cream.

5. The dough should feel light and be a little sticky. Place a handful of it on a lightly floured surface to shape into a 4-inch square about ¾ inch thick.

6. Cut the square from corner to corner twice to make four triangles. Repeat with the remaining dough to make as many scones as the dough provides.

7. Mix the egg and vanilla together in a small bowl. Either quickly dunk each scone in the wash or use a pastry brush to dab the top and sides.

8. Place the scones on the prepared baking sheet and sprinkle the tops with turbinado sugar and a tiny pinch of sea salt.

9. Bake for about 15 minutes, or until the scones are lightly browned on the sides and golden across the top. Cool on racks for 5 minutes before serving.

CHERRY-WALNUT SCONES

Heavy cream	½ cup
Vanilla extract	½ teaspoon
Unbleached all-purpose flour	10 ounces (2 cups)
Dried cherries, chopped	½ cup
Walnuts, chopped	½ cup
Granulated sugar	¼ cup
Turbinado sugar	¼ cup, plus extra for sprinkling
Baking powder	1½ teaspoons
Salt	¾ teaspoon, plus extra for sprinkling
Unsalted butter, very cold	4 ounces (1 stick)
Egg	1
Kirsch (cherry liqueur)	1 teaspoon (optional)
Vanilla extract or bourbon	½ teaspoon

Dried cherries and walnuts make a happy couple. A lovely aroma fills the kitchen when these are in the oven.

1. Preheat the oven to 375°F and place a rack in the middle. Line a baking sheet with parchment paper or a silicone baking mat.

2. In a small bowl, combine the cream and vanilla and set aside. In a large bowl, combine the flour, cherries, walnuts, sugars, baking powder, and salt. Whisk for about 10 seconds; set aside.

3. Cut the butter into small pieces, then cut the pieces into the flour mixture using your fingers, a fork, or a stand mixer fitted with the paddle attachment set on low speed. Once the flour and butter clump together when pinched, slowly add the cream mixture a little at a time while turning the dough. Stop when the dough easily forms a ball—it may not be necessary to use all of the cream.

4. The dough should feel light and barely moist. Place a handful on a lightly floured surfaced to shape into a 4-inch square about ¾ inch thick.

5. Cut the square from corner to corner twice to make four triangles. Repeat with the remaining dough to make as many scones as possible.

6. Mix the egg, kirsch, if using, and vanilla in a small bowl. Either quickly dunk each scone in the wash or use a pastry brush to dab the top and sides. Place the scones on the prepared baking sheet and sprinkle the tops with turbinado sugar and a tiny pinch of sea salt.

7. Bake for about 15 minutes, or until the scones are lightly browned on the sides and golden across the top. Cool on racks for 5 minutes before serving.

MULTIGRAIN RUM RAISIN SCONES

Whole rolled oats	5 tablespoons
Flax seeds	1 tablespoon
Kosher salt	½ teaspoon
Sea salt	½ teaspoon, plus extra for sprinkling
Unbleached all-purpose flour	7 ounces (1⅓ cups)
Whole-wheat flour	2 tablespoons
Currants or raisins	⅓ cup
Pecans, roasted	⅓ cup
Turbinado or granulated sugar	3 tablespoons, plus extra for sprinkling
Millet	2 tablespoons
Cornmeal	2 teaspoons
Cream of tartar	1 teaspoon
Baking soda	½ teaspoon
Unsalted butter, very cold	4 ounces (1 stick)
Low-fat milk	2 to 4 tablespoons
Egg	1
Rum	¼ teaspoon

The combination of whole grains in these scones creates a bouquet of flavor that blends nicely with the rum and dried fruit—and unlike many whole-grain products, these are very tender to the bite. Although either works well in this recipe, I prefer currants to the larger raisins, which can end up dominating.

1. Preheat the oven to 375°F and place a rack in the middle. Line a baking sheet with parchment paper or a silicone baking mat.

2. Grind 3 tablespoons of the oats, the flax, and salts to a fine powder in a spice grinder. In a large bowl, combine them with the flours, currants, pecans, sugar, millet, cornmeal, cream of tartar, and baking soda. Whisk for about 10 seconds and set aside.

3. Cut the butter into small pieces, then cut the pieces into the flour mixture using your fingers, a fork, or a stand mixer fitted with the paddle attachment set on low speed. Once the flour and butter clump together when pinched, slowly add the milk a little at a time while turning the dough. Stop when the dough easily forms a ball—it may not be necessary to use all of the milk.

4. The dough should feel light but moist and slightly tacky. Place a handful of it on a lightly floured surface to shape into a 4-inch square about ¾ inch thick.

5. Cut the square from corner to corner twice to make four triangles. Repeat with the remaining dough to make as many scones as the dough provides.

6. Mix the egg and rum together in a small bowl. Either quickly dunk each scone in the wash or use a pastry brush to dab the tops and sides.

7. Place the scones on the prepared baking sheet and sprinkle the tops with turbinado sugar and a tiny pinch of sea salt.

8. Bake for about 15 minutes, or until the scones are lightly browned on the sides and golden across the top. Cool on racks for 5 minutes before serving.

If you use a substitute for the cream, be sure to eat the scones when they're hot, either right out of the oven or reheated in the toaster. They won't be quite as tender as those made with cream, but this is a small sacrifice for fewer calories.

GINGER-PECAN SCONES

Unbleached all-purpose flour	10 ounces (2 cups)
Granulated sugar	4 ounces (½ cup)
Turbinado sugar	2 tablespoons, plus extra for sprinkling
Baking powder	1 teaspoon
Ground ginger	1 tablespoon
Kosher salt	½ teaspoon
Sea salt	½ teaspoon, plus extra for sprinkling
Unsalted butter, very cold	5 ounces (1 stick 2 tablespoons)
Pecan halves	½ cup
Crystallized ginger pieces	½ cup
Heavy cream	up to ¾ cup
Egg	1
Vanilla extract	¼ teaspoon

These are the best-selling scones at CakeLove. I've been known to frequently snag one from the rack when no one is looking. I love 'em toasted with peach preserves. Unlike other recipes, I recommend folding the pecans and crystallized ginger into the dough after the butter is worked into the flour mixture. Adding the pecans earlier will distribute too much oil into the dough, which makes the resulting scones too flat and heavy tasting.

1. Preheat the oven to 375°F and place a rack in the middle. Line a baking sheet with parchment paper or a silicone baking mat.

2. In a large bowl mix, combine the flour, sugars, baking powder, ground ginger, and salts. Whisk for about 10 seconds and set aside.

3. Cut the butter into small pieces, then cut the pieces into the flour mixture using your fingers, a fork, or a stand mixer fitted with the paddle attachment set on low speed. Once the flour and butter clump together when pinched, stir in the pecans and crystallized ginger pieces.

4. Next, slowly add the cream a little at a time while turning the dough. Stop when the dough easily forms a ball—it may not be necessary to use all of the cream.

5. The dough should feel light and barely moist. Place a handful of it on a lightly floured surface to shape into a 4-inch square about ¾ inch thick.

6. Cut the square from corner to corner twice to make four triangles. Repeat with the remaining dough to make as many scones as the dough provides.

7. Mix the egg and vanilla together in a small bowl. Either quickly dunk each scone in the wash or use a pastry brush to dab the top and sides.

8. Place the scones on the prepared baking sheet and sprinkle the tops with turbinado sugar and a tiny pinch of sea salt.

9. Bake for about 15 minutes, or until the scones are lightly browned on the sides and golden across the top. Cool on wire racks for 5 minutes before serving.

MULTIGRAIN SCONES

Whole rolled oats	¼ cup
Flax seeds	1 tablespoon
Unbleached all-purpose flour	10 ounces (2 cups)
Whole-wheat pastry flour	¼ cup
Pecans, roasted	½ cup
Dried cranberries	⅓ cup
Cornmeal	2 tablespoons
Lemon zest	1½ teaspoons
Cream of tartar	½ teaspoon
Baking soda	¼ teaspoon
Sea salt	¼ teaspoon, plus extra for sprinkling
Fleur de sel	¼ teaspoon
Unsalted butter, very cold	3 ounces (¾ stick)
Low-fat milk	up to ¼ cup
Egg	1
Vanilla extract	¼ teaspoon
Turbinado sugar	for sprinkling

Here is a lighter scone for those who want to eliminate the extra calories that come from heavy cream. The texture is a little crumbly, but they're still very tasty.

1. Preheat the oven to 375°F and place a rack in the middle. Line a baking sheet with parchment paper or a silicone baking mat.

2. Grind the oats and flax to a fine powder in a spice grinder. In a large bowl, combine them with the flours, pecans, cranberries, cornmeal, zest, cream of tartar, baking soda, and salts. Whisk for about 10 seconds and set aside.

3. Cut the butter into small pieces, then cut the pieces into the flour mixture using your fingers, a fork, or a stand mixer fitted with the paddle attachment set on low speed. Once the flour and butter clump together when pinched, slowly add the milk while turning the dough. Stop when the dough forms a ball—not all of the liquid may be necessary.

4. The dough should feel light but moist, and almost wet. Place a handful on a lightly floured surface to shape into a 4-inch square about ¾ inch thick.

5. Cut the square from corner to corner twice to make four triangles. Repeat with the remaining dough to make as many scones as the dough provides.

6. Mix the egg and vanilla in a small bowl. Quickly dunk each scone in the wash or use a pastry brush to dab the top and sides. Place the scones on the prepared baking sheet and sprinkle with turbinado sugar and a pinch of sea salt.

7. Bake for about 15 minutes, or until the scones are lightly browned on the sides and golden across the top. Cool on racks for 5 minutes before serving.

MINT-ALMOND SCONES

There's something about the scent of mint with the almonds that makes this combination feel even more buttery than it is. Add a splash of bourbon to bring out flavors reminiscent of a mint julep—never a bad cocktail for brunch!

1. Preheat the oven to 375° and place a rack in middle. Line a baking sheet with parchment paper or a silicone baking mat.

2. In a large bowl, combine the flours, sugars, baking powder, kosher salt, mint, and almonds. Whisk for about 10 seconds and set aside.

3. Cut the butter into small pieces, then cut them into the flour mix using your fingers, a fork, or a stand mixer fitted with the paddle attachment set on low speed. Once the mixture clumps together when pinched, slowly add the half-and-half or milk while turning the dough. Stop when the dough forms a ball—not all of the liquid may be necessary.

4. The dough should feel light and barely moist. Place a handful of it on a lightly floured surface to shape into a 4-inch square that's about ¾ inch thick.

5. Cut the square from corner to corner twice to make four triangles. Repeat with the remaining dough to make as many scones as the dough provides.

6. Mix the egg and vanilla extract or bourbon together in a bowl. Either quickly dunk each scone in the wash or use a pastry brush to dab the top and sides.

7. Place the scones on the prepared baking sheet and sprinkle the tops with turbinado or granulated sugar to taste and a tiny pinch of sea salt. Bake for about 15 minutes or until the scones are lightly browned on the sides and golden across the top. Cool on racks for 5 minutes before serving.

Unbleached all-purpose flour	7½ ounces (1¼ cups)
Whole-wheat flour	1¼ ounces (¼ cup)
Baking powder	1 teaspoon
Kosher salt	½ teaspoon
Granulated sugar	¼ cup, plus extra for sprinkling (optional)
Turbinado sugar	2 tablespoons, plus extra for sprinkling (optional)
Fresh mint, finely minced	1 tablespoon
Sliced almonds	6 tablespoons
Unsalted butter, very cold	3 ounces (¾ stick)
Half-and-half or milk	about ⅓ cup
Egg	1
Vanilla extract or bourbon	dash
Sea salt	for sprinkling

BISCUITS

Biscuits don't have to be something to fret about. Getting them to rise is a cinch, and keeping the center tender and the edges crusty takes nothing but a light touch when handling the dough. Like scones, I find that biscuits can carry a variety of flavors, so once you get the basics down, try adding different herbs and spices, cheeses, and sweeteners to the mix.

CUT YOUR BISCUITS with a proper biscuit cutter with a sharp edge. Cut straight down and don't twist the cutter. Lift it and poke the dough through to remove the biscuit.

MAKE THE CUTS ALMOST SEAMLESS in order to get as many cuts as possible from the first shaped disc. Wipe and clean any dough off of the cutter between cuts.

DO NOT OVERMIX your ingredients and handle the dough as little as possible.

USE VERY COLD BUTTER—return it to the fridge after you've cut it into small pieces and keep it there until you're ready to use it.

MY BASIC BISCUIT

Best served hot and fresh from the oven, these biscuits are light, airy, and delicate. They're easy to throw together and bake quickly. You can make them extra rich by brushing them with melted butter before baking. This will give you crispy edges. I like to spread the tops with honey or jam right after they're out of the oven.

Unbleached all-purpose flour	13 ounces (about 2½ cups)
Sugar	¼ cup
Cream of tartar	2 teaspoons
Baking soda	1 teaspoon
Sea salt	1 teaspoon
Unsalted butter, very cold	4 ounces (1 stick)
Half-and-half	1½ cups
Unsalted butter, melted	3 ounces (¾ stick) (optional)

1. Preheat the oven to 375°F and place a rack in the middle. Line a baking sheet with parchment paper or a silicone baking mat.

2. In the bowl of a stand mixer fitted with the paddle attachment, combine the flour, sugar, cream of tartar, baking soda, and salt. Mix for 30 seconds on low.

3. Cut the cold butter into small pieces and add them to the flour mixture with the mixer on low speed. Continue mixing until the mixture holds together when pinched, about 30 seconds.

4. Drizzle in the half-and-half until the dough is a wet, slightly pasty mass. You may not need all the liquid.

5. Turn out the dough onto a floured work surface. Dust your hands well with flour. Lightly knead by hand and shape the dough into a disc ½ to ¾ inch thick.

6. With a 2- to 3-inch biscuit cutter, cut as many biscuits as the dough will provide. Gently reform any scraps into biscuits without cutting. Brush the tops with melted butter, if desired, and place them on the prepared baking sheet.

7. Bake for 12 to 15 minutes, or until the biscuits are lightly browned on the bottom. Allow to cool for 5 minutes on the baking sheet before serving. Store in an airtight container and reheat in a toaster oven.

ADDING A PINCH OF FLAVOR

I often jazz up my biscuits by adding a sprinkle of sugar, spices, or herbs to the flour that I use on my work surface when kneading the dough. It adds a subtle but special touch of flavor.

GRAVY FOR BISCUITS

Hailing from the South isn't a prerequisite for appreciating this staple found on many breakfast menus below the Mason–Dixon line. The gravy uses sausage and bacon drippings rather than butter, and milk in lieu of stock.

Makes 2 cups

Sausage **4 links**

Bacon **2 strips**

Unbleached all-purpose flour **2 tablespoons**

Milk, at room temperature **1½ cups**

Salt **to taste**

Freshly ground black pepper **to taste**

1. Pan-fry the bacon and sausage until cooked through, but not crispy, in a large, heavy-bottomed skillet. Remove the meat and set it aside.

2. Pour off the pan drippings and return about ¼ cup to the pan. Keep the pan hot over medium to high heat, then quickly stir in the flour to make a roux.

3. Continue to push the roux around the pan to cook the flour until it darkens to a medium blond.

4. When the roux reaches the color you want and smells nutty, briskly whisk in the milk. Continue to whisk the gravy as it simmers and thickens. Add salt and pepper to taste.

5. To serve, split biscuits on the plate and pour the gravy over. Serve the meat on the side.

LIGHTER-THAN-AIR BISCUITS

These biscuits practically melt in your mouth. Sweet white rice flour makes them super light and adds a touch of sweetness as well. It's easy to find in the specialty baking aisle of major grocery stores. I like Bob's Red Mill brand; the rice is milled to a very fine powder with no grittiness.

Unbleached all-purpose flour	10 ounces (2 cups)
Sweet rice flour	6 ounces (⅔ cup)
Sugar	3 tablespoons
Cream of tartar	1½ teaspoons
Sea salt	1¼ teaspoons
Baking soda	¾ teaspoon
Unsalted butter, very cold	3 ounces (¾ stick)
Half-and-half	1½ cups
Unsalted butter, melted	3 ounces (¾ stick) (optional)

1. Preheat the oven to 375°F and place a rack in the middle. Line a baking sheet with parchment paper or a silicone baking mat.

2. In the bowl of a stand mixer fitted with the paddle attachment, combine the flours, sugar, cream of tartar, salt, and baking soda. Mix for 30 seconds on low.

3. Cut the cold butter into small pieces and add them to the flour mixture with the mixer on low speed. Continue mixing until the mixture holds together when pinched, about 30 seconds.

4. Drizzle in the half-and-half until the dough is a wet, slightly pasty mass. You may not need all the liquid.

5. Turn out the dough onto a floured work surface. Dust your hands well with flour. Lightly knead by hand and shape the dough into a disc ½ to ¾ inch thick.

6. With a 2- to 3-inch biscuit cutter, cut as many biscuits as the dough will provide. Gently re-form the scraps into biscuits without cutting. Quickly dunk the tops of the biscuits in melted butter, if desired, and place them on the prepared baking sheet.

7. Bake for 12 to 15 minutes, or until the biscuits are lightly browned on the bottom. Allow to cool for 5 minutes on the baking sheet before serving. Store in an airtight container and reheat in a toaster oven.

Many Southern bakers are passionate about using soft winter-wheat flour for their biscuits and are especially devoted to the White Lily brand. These flours have less protein and will produce a lighter biscuit. I've used White Lily plenty of times, and it's just great for biscuits. If you can't find it in your area, try working with a very light, low-protein pastry flour.

THYME-PEPPER BISCUITS

Unbleached all-purpose flour	10 ounces (2 cups)
Lemon zest	3 tablespoons
Fresh thyme, chopped	2 tablespoons
Baking powder	1 tablespoon
Superfine sugar	1 tablespoon
Sea salt	¾ teaspoon
Freshly ground black pepper	1 tablespoon
Unsalted butter, very cold	4 ounces (1 stick)
Heavy cream	1 cup
Unsalted butter, melted	3 ounces (¾ stick) (optional)
Egg	1
Vanilla extract	splash (optional)

SMOKED CHEDDAR AND SAGE BISCUITS

Prepare as you would Thyme–Pepper Biscuits, adding 2 tablespoons minced fresh sage, ⅓ cup grated smoked cheddar cheese, and 3 pinches of your favorite variety of paprika in place of the thyme and lemon zest.

These biscuits were often a part of staff breakfasts in our first year at CakeLove. They're light and fluffy platforms for scrambled eggs or a wad of honey-butter.

1. Preheat the oven to 400°F and place a rack in the middle. Line a baking sheet with parchment paper or a silicone baking mat.

2. In a medium bowl, whisk to combine the flour, zest, thyme, baking powder, sugar, salt, and pepper.

3. Cut the butter into small pieces, then use a fork to cut the pieces into the flour until the mixture resembles a coarse meal. (You can also complete steps 2 and 3 with a food processor or stand mixer.)

4. Make a well in the middle of the flour-butter mixture and add the cream. Using a flexible spatula, fold in the cream until it comes together to form a sticky dough.

5. Transfer the dough to a lightly floured surface and—with fingers dusted with flour—shape it into a 1-inch-high disc.

6. Use a 3-inch biscuit cutter to cut as many biscuits as the dough will provide. Gently re-form the scraps into biscuits without cutting. Quickly dunk the tops of the biscuits in melted butter, if desired, and place them on the prepared baking sheet. Alternatively, in a small bowl, whisk together the egg and vanilla and brush it on the biscuit tops to add color and shine.

7. Bake for 20 minutes, or until the biscuits are lightly browned on the bottom. Allow to cool for 5 minutes on the baking sheet before serving. Store in an airtight container and reheat in a toaster oven.

SWEET POTATO BISCUITS

Sweet potatoes	2 small (10 ounces)
Unsalted butter, soft	4 ounces (1 stick)
Orange zest	1 teaspoon
Unbleached all-purpose flour	8 ounces (about 1½ cup)
Sugar	2 tablespoons, plus extra for sprinkling
Cream of tartar	2 teaspoons
Baking soda	1 teaspoon
Sea salt	1 teaspoon
Ground cinnamon	pinch
Orange juice	4 tablespoons
Half-and-half	4 tablespoons
Unsalted butter, melted	3 ounces (¾ stick) (optional)

Make sure your baking soda and baking powder are fresh. Check the date for freshness, and if you have any doubts, drop the soda in vinegar or lemon juice and the powder in water. Bubbles tell you it's still good.

My sister Lenora makes the best sweet potato biscuits at Thanksgiving—I usually plow through four or five in one sitting. Her recipe remains a secret, but this is a close adaptation. Plan ahead and throw in a couple of sweet potatoes the next time the oven is on. Once baked, they'll keep in the fridge for a few days until you're ready to make your biscuits.

There isn't a lot of liquid in this recipe and a lot of the orange flavor comes from the zest. If you want a more tender biscuit, omit the orange juice and double the half-and-half, or be indulgent and swap in heavy cream.

1. Preheat the oven to 375°F and place a rack in the middle. Line a baking sheet with parchment paper or a silicone baking mat.

2. Roast the sweet potatoes on a cookie sheet until soft all the way through the middle. Allow to cool completely before scooping out the flesh.

3. In the bowl of a stand mixer fitted with the paddle attachment, mash together the sweet potato, soft butter, and zest on low to medium speed for 3 minutes.

4. In a large bowl, whisk together the flour, sugar, cream of tartar, baking soda, salt, and cinnamon, then add them to the potato mixture.

5. On low speed, slowly drizzle in the orange juice, followed by the half-and-half, until the dough is a wet mass. Note that it will be very wet—some of the half-and-half may not be needed. Increase the speed to medium and mix for 15 seconds to develop the gluten.

6. Turn out the dough onto a floured work surface. Gently shape by hand into a disc ¾ inch thick.

7. With a 2- to 3-inch biscuit cutter, cut as many biscuits as the dough will provide. Gently re-form the scraps into biscuits without cutting; otherwise, there's too much waste. Quickly dunk the tops of the biscuits in melted butter, if desired, and place them on the prepared baking sheet. Sprinkle with a pinch of sugar.

8. Bake for about 15 minutes, or until the biscuits are lightly browned on the bottom. Allow to cool for 5 minutes on the baking sheet before serving. Store in an airtight container and reheat in a toaster oven.

Most of my biscuit recipes call for baking soda and cream of tartar because I want a fresh combination of acid and alkaline to give maximum lift to the dough. A fresh baking powder will do the same job and I can't notice a difference in taste, but I find that I just get better results using tartar and soda. If you want to make your own baking powder, follow a ratio of one part baking soda to two parts cream of tartar.

OATMEAL

One of the great benefits of our renewed appreciation of whole grains is the return of hot cereals for breakfast. To me, there is nothing better than a bowl of creamy porridge to make the body feel nourished in all the right ways. Hot oatmeal—especially on a cold, dreary day—picks me up, warms my tum, and fuels me for the daily adventures of being a dad. There are lots of ways...

TYPES OF OATMEAL

Rolled oats are made from whole grain oats that have been flattened and steamed. Quick-cooking varieties are available, but stick with the type often described as "old-fashioned" for a richer taste and texture. I like old-fashioned rolled oats. They do double-duty in baked goods and pancakes, so there's just less to stock in the pantry. Buy them in bulk from a quality grocer and you'll save a bundle on one of the most versatile cereal grains available. To get the proper creamy texture, use a combination of water and milk in a two-to-one proportion of liquid to oats and then cook them low and slow.

Steel-cut oats, also known as Irish oatmeal, are the same whole grain oats that have been steel cut rather than rolled, and haven't been steamed. They take longer to cook and have a chewier texture than rolled oats.

CLASSIC OATMEAL

Porridge is good enough on its own, but adding a handful of nuts or dried fruit or even a sliced banana always goes over well. Whenever I use honey in hot cereal, I prefer raw or crystalized honeys. They taste sweeter, have less moisture, offer benefits of helpful bacteria (but potentially harmful to infants), and pack a lot of flavor. Whenever you can, try out raw or artisanal honeys for a tasty new experience.

Whole rolled oats	1 cup
Milk or soy milk	1 cup
Sea salt	a pinch
Raw honey	2 tablespoons
Vanilla extract	1 teaspoon

1. Combine the oats, milk, 1 cup water, sea salt, honey, and vanilla in a 1-quart saucepan and bring to a simmer over medium heat.

2. Reduce the heat to low, loosely cover, and cook without stirring for about 10 minutes, or until the oatmeal thickens to your desired consistency.

3. Serve with milk and dried or fresh berries.

APPLE-CRANBERRY OATMEAL

Unsalted butter	1 tablespoon
Apple (your favorite local variety)	1 peeled and cut into ½-inch dice
Whole rolled oats	1 cup
Apple cider	1 cup
Cranberries, dried	½ cup
Sugar	2 tablespoons
Ground cinnamon	¼ teaspoon

Make the morning a little brighter with a new twist on the old-school classic. Fresh, diced apples mean a lot, but the cider makes the difference. This is perfect for fall mornings when freshly pressed apple cider is at its peak.

1. Heat a 1-quart saucepan over medium heat. Add the butter and apples and sauté for about 3 minutes.

2. Add the oats, 1 cup water, the cider, cranberries, sugar, and cinnamon and bring to a simmer.

3. Reduce the heat to low and loosely cover. Cook without stirring for about 10 minutes, or until the oatmeal thickens to your desired consistency.

4. Serve with milk and your choice of sweetener, if desired.

CHAI OATMEAL

Soy milk	½ cup
Milk	½ cup
Honey	2 tablespoons
Cinnamon sticks	2
Nutmeg, freshly ground	½ teaspoon
Star anise	1 star
Green cardamom pods, unopened	5 to 8
Whole rolled oats	1 cup

All of the traditional chai spices pair wonderfully with oats. Because we're steeping the spices in the milk, it's not necessary to remove the cardamom seeds from the pods, grate the cinnamon, or crush the star anise.

1. In a 1-quart saucepan over medium heat, combine 1 cup water, the milks, honey, cinnamon, nutmeg, star anise, and cardamom. Bring to a simmer, and then turn off the heat and steep the spices for 10 minutes.

2. Strain out the spices and return the milk to the same pot. Add the oats and bring to a simmer over medium heat.

3. Reduce the heat to low and loosely cover. Cook without stirring for about 10 minutes, or until the oatmeal thickens to your desired consistency.

4. Serve with milk and sweetener of choice, if desired.

Store-bought ground nutmeg loses almost all its flavor well before it makes it to the grocery store shelves, so make it a practice to buy nutmeg whole and just grate it on a Microplane.

BANANA–GINGER OATMEAL

This is one of the easiest gourmet breakfasts I can make.
It's a one-pot wonder that cooks slowly while my wife and
I get our daughter ready for school. The flaxseeds are
optional but lend a more wholesome feel to a breakfast
that's already healthy.

Crystalized ginger	¼ to ½ cup
Whole rolled oats	1 cup
Milk or soy milk	1 cup
Banana, peeled and sliced	1 medium (about ¾ cup)
Flaxseeds	1 tablespoon
Honey	1 tablespoon
Salt	a pinch
Sugar	1 tablespoon (optional)

1. Chop the crystalized ginger into small pieces. Rinse the
   sugar off them if you're watching your glucose levels.

2. Put all of the ingredients in a 1-quart saucepan with 1¼ cup
   water and stir to combine.

3. Cook over low to medium heat until the oatmeal simmers
   lightly, about 15 minutes.

4. Serve with sliced strawberries and honey, if desired.

QUICK BREADS, STICKY BUNS, AND CAKES

Which came first: brunch or the heavenly baked goods that bring to mind a lazy Sunday afternoon? Although the steps are easy, these are not everyday recipes. Rest assured, though, that gooey, yeasty rolls, flavor-filled sweet loaves, and delicate cakes are worth the weekly wait.

QUICK BREADS

If there's any type of baking that lends itself to creativity, it's quick breads. These recipes are versatile and very forgiving. You can pretty safely substitute any fruit or vegetable as long as the same preparation method is maintained. While developing these recipes, I tried lots of crazy swaps: yellow squash for zucchini, pears instead of apples, and one type of nut for another. As their name implies, these breads come together in short order without a lot of fuss. They also freeze well, so it's easy to have a couple of loaves on hand and ready to reheat for a weekday breakfast.

ALWAYS GREASE the loaf pan well.

USE A WOODEN SPOON or spatula and mix by hand rather than with a mixer.

DO NOT OVERMIX. As the name implies, the batter comes together quickly. There should still be dry patches when it's poured into the pan.

USE A LOAF PAN with sides that flare out at an angle. Straight-sided pans put too much pressure on the batter while it bakes, which causes overflow and makes the crumb tight.

APPLE BREAD

**Any discussion of quick breads wouldn't be complete
without apple bread.** Wet, messy, and delicious, you almost
need a fork to eat this one. It's a perfect bread to bake in the
early fall, when the apple harvest first hits the local farmers market. You'll love the aroma of spices that fill the house
when this is in the oven. Slice and serve it plain, or with
honey and Cream Cheese Drizzle (page 50).

Apples, peeled and grated	3 cups
Superfine sugar	4 ounces (½ cup)
Eggs	4
Unsalted butter, melted	2 ounces (½ stick)
Vegetable oil	¼ cup
Vanilla extract	1 teaspoon
Unbleached all-purpose flour	7 ounces (1¼ cups)
Walnuts	½ cup
Light brown sugar	¼ cup, packed
Baking powder	1 teaspoon
Salt	¼ teaspoon
Ground cinnamon	½ teaspoon
Nutmeg, freshly grated (optional)	½ teaspoon
Ground allspice (optional)	¼ teaspoon
Anise seeds (optional)	¼ teaspoon

1. Preheat the oven to 350°F and place a rack in the middle.
   Coat an 8½-inch loaf pan with nonstick baking spray. Set
   aside.

2. In a large bowl, toss the apples with 2 tablespoons of the
   superfine sugar. Add the eggs, butter, oil, and vanilla and
   stir to combine.

3. In a separate large bowl, stir to combine the flour, walnuts,
   remaining superfine sugar, brown sugar, baking powder,
   salt, cinnamon, and nutmeg, allspice, and anise, if using.

4. Gently fold the liquid ingredients into the dry ingredients
   with a flexible spatula.

5. Spoon the batter into the prepared loaf pan—no need to
   smooth out the top.

6. Bake for 45 to 50 minutes, or until the top is golden and a
   wooden skewer inserted in the center comes out clean.

7. Let the bread cool for 5 minutes, then gently tip it out to
   cool on a wire rack.

ZUCCHINI BREAD

Gala apples, peeled and grated	2 cups
Zucchini, grated	2 cups
Superfine sugar	5 ounces (½ cup plus 2 tablespoons)
Unsalted butter, melted	2 ounces (½ stick)
Vegetable oil	¼ cup
Eggs	2
Molasses	1 tablespoon
Vanilla extract	1 teaspoon
Pecans or walnuts, roasted and hand crushed	1 cup
Unbleached all-purpose flour	4 ounces (¾ cup)
Whole-wheat pastry flour	2 tablespoons
Whole rolled oats	1 ounce (¼ cup)
Cornmeal	1 tablespoon
Baking powder	1 teaspoon
Salt	½ teaspoon
Ground cinnamon	½ teaspoon
Confectioners' sugar	for dusting (optional)

Make use of summer's bounty with this easy and reliable loaf bread. The peppery roasted pecans add a great hint of spice. Don't worry about precise measurements of the zucchini and apple. Going long or short on either one is okay so long as together they measure 4 cups total.

1. Preheat the oven to 325°F and place a rack in the middle. Coat an 8½-inch loaf pan with nonstick baking spray. Set aside.

2. In a medium bowl, toss together the apples, zucchini, and ¼ cup of the sugar.

3. Add the butter, oil, eggs, molasses, and vanilla. Stir just to combine. In a separate large bowl, stir to combine the nuts, flours, oats, cornmeal, remaining superfine sugar, the baking powder, salt, and cinnamon.

4. Gently fold the liquid ingredients into the dry ingredients with a flexible spatula.

5. Spoon the batter into the prepared loaf pan and gently smooth out the top.

6. Bake for about 50 minutes, or until a wooden skewer inserted in the center comes out clean and the top lightly bounces back when tapped.

7. Let the bread cool for 5 minutes, then gently tip it out to cool on a wire rack. Dust the top lightly with confectioners' sugar, if desired.

BANANA BREAD

Loved for its simplicity and thrifty nature, banana bread should never be underestimated. There's a reason everyone loves it! I dig finding big chunks of bananas in banana bread, so I use ripe, yellow fruit and only mash it halfway instead of to a pulp. Use agave nectar if you want a sweetener with less of a sugary punch.

1. Preheat the oven to 325°F and place a rack in the middle. Coat an 8½-inch loaf pan with nonstick baking spray. Set aside.

2. Mash the bananas in a bowl, leaving some chunks, then add the oil, butter, eggs, honey or agave, and vanilla and stir to lightly combine.

3. In a large bowl, whisk together the flours, nuts, sugar, cornmeal, baking powder, salt, and cinnamon. Gently fold the wet ingredients into the dry ingredients.

4. Pour the batter into the prepared loaf pan and gently smooth the top with a spatula.

5. Bake for about 55 minutes, or until a wooden skewer inserted in the center comes out clean and the top lightly bounces back when tapped.

6. Let the bread cool for 5 minutes, then gently tip it out to cool on a wire rack.

DECADENT CHOCOLATE-CHUNK BANANA BREAD

Say good-bye to self-control when you add up to 1 cup of dime-size chocolate chunks to the dry ingredients. After the batter is in the pan, push any visible pieces of chocolate underneath the batter; otherwise they'll burn.

Bananas	2 large
Vegetable oil	¼ cup
Unsalted butter	2 ounces (½ stick), melted
Eggs	2
Honey or agave nectar	3 tablespoons
Vanilla extract	1 teaspoon
Unbleached all-purpose flour	6½ ounces (1¼ cups)
Whole-wheat pastry flour	3 ounces (½ cup)
Walnuts or pecans, roasted and crushed	1 cup
Superfine sugar	2 ounces (¼ cup)
Cornmeal	1 tablespoon
Baking powder	1 teaspoon
Salt	¾ teaspoon
Ground cinnamon	¼ teaspoon

APPLE-CARROT BREAD

A dose of freshly grated ginger skips across the tongue in this lightly sweetened quick bread, which draws subtle flavor from a delicate balance of whole wheat, pecans, apples, and carrots. It's a healthful addition to any brunch. I like it served warm with butter and honey.

1. Preheat the oven to 325°F and place a rack in the middle. Coat an 8½-inch loaf pan with nonstick baking spray. Set aside.

2. In a large bowl, combine the carrots, apples, superfine sugar, and ginger. Add the butter, oil, eggs, honey, and molasses. Lightly stir to combine.

3. In another large bowl, stir to combine the flours, pecans (if using), brown sugar, baking powder, salt, and cinnamon.

4. Gently fold the liquid ingredients into the dry ingredients with a flexible spatula.

5. Spoon the batter into the prepared loaf pan and gently smooth out the top with a spatula.

6. Bake for about 50 minutes, or until a wooden skewer inserted in the center comes out clean and the top lightly bounces when tapped.

7. Let the bread cool for 5 minutes, then gently tip it out to cool on a wire rack.

Carrots, peeled and grated	1½ cups
Apples, peeled and grated	½ cup
Superfine sugar	4 ounces (½ cup)
Fresh ginger, peeled and grated	1 tablespoon
Unsalted butter, melted	2 ounces (½ stick)
Vegetable oil	¼ cup
Eggs	2
Honey	2 tablespoons
Molasses	1 teaspoon
Unbleached all-purpose flour	4 ounces (¾ cup)
Whole-wheat pastry flour	3 ounces (½ cup)
Roasted pecans, crushed (optional)	¾ cup
Light brown sugar	¼ cup, packed
Baking powder	1 teaspoon
Salt	½ teaspoon
Ground cinnamon	½ teaspoon

QUICK HOME-SPUN CORNBREAD

Cornmeal	2 ounces (½ cup)
Unbleached all-purpose flour	2 ounces (about ½ cup)
Superfine sugar	3 tablespoons
Baking powder	½ teaspoon
Salt	¼ teaspoon, plus ⅛ teaspoon
Milk	½ cup
Eggs	2
Vegetable oil	1 tablespoon
Vanilla extract	½ teaspoon
Fresh corn	1 or 2 ears (about 1 to 1½ cups kernels)
Unsalted butter	2 tablespoons
Jalapeño-Honey Butter (page 49)	for serving

This recipe harkens back to my days in grad school, when I shared a house on T Street in DC. I found myself in the kitchen a lot more than I should have been; it was always much more fun to cook and hang out than study—imagine that! My housemates and I would sit around the kitchen every weekend morning recounting the adventures of the night before, sopping up Jalapeño-Honey Butter with thick wedges of cornbread and bacon. Unlike true Southern cornbread, this is slightly sweet. It could easily be baked as muffins instead of in a pan.

1. Preheat the oven to 400°F and place a rack in the middle. Grease a 9-by-13-inch baking dish with oil or melted butter. Set aside.

2. In a large bowl, whisk together the cornmeal, flour, sugar, baking powder, and salt. In a small bowl, beat together the milk, eggs, oil, and vanilla.

3. Remove the husk and silk from the corn and carefully slice off the kernels with a chef's knife. Melt the butter in a small frying pan. Add the kernels and sauté over medium heat for about 3 minutes.

4. Stir the wet ingredients into the dry and fold in the kernels. Pour into the prepared baking dish.

5. Bake for about 25 minutes, or until a skewer inserted in the center comes out clean and the top lightly bounces back when tapped.

6. Let the cornbread rest out of the oven for at least 10 minutes before serving with Jalapeño-Honey Butter.

STICKY BUNS

Unveil a basket of freshly baked sticky buns and watch the smiles appear. Although they look complicated, these are way easier to make than you might think—it's just a matter of timing. Making sticky buns requires a good two- to three-hour commitment, but there's plenty of downtime so you can take care of other things. The dough is rich and yeasty, meaning that it will stand well on its own or hold up to endless flavorful additions.

WATCH THE TEMPERATURE of the milk when adding the yeast—you don't want it to be too high or it will kill the bacteria.

LOOSELY COVER the dough and proof it in a warm, draft-free area. Whenever I've tried proofing the dough in a space lower than 90°F, it does not rise.

CHECK THE DATE on the package of yeast you're using for your sticky buns—if the yeast has expired, don't use it. Old yeast won't rise and the buns will be flat and dense. To be safe, you should also store yeast in the fridge.

ROLL A TIGHT LOG when making the cinnamon roll and use a very sharp knife to cut through it.

THIS IS A LIGHT AND FRAGILE DOUGH; don't over work it. Knead gently.

CINNAMON ROLLS

FOR THE ROLLS

Milk	1 cup
Active dry yeast	1 (1.75-ounce) package
Superfine sugar	4 ounces (½ cup)
Unbleached all-purpose flour	20 ounces (4 cups), plus extra as needed
Unsalted butter, soft	3 ounces (¾ stick)
Eggs	2
Table or sea salt	1 teaspoon

FOR THE FILLING

Dark brown sugar	1 cup, packed
Unsalted butter, soft	6 ounces (1½ sticks)
Ground cinnamon	1 tablespoon

FOR THE WASH

Egg	1
Milk	2 tablespoons
Vanilla extract	¼ teaspoon

FOR THE FROSTING

Cream Cheese Drizzle (page 50)	1 batch

There's no more recognizable breakfast treat that is welcomed at any time of day than cinnamon rolls. They are synonymous with taking a break to spend some time licking frosting off your fingers. When shopping for ingredients, read the labels to be sure you're picking up real cinnamon, not cassia, which is often labeled "cinnamon"— it's not, and it's much less flavorful.

1. In a small saucepan, warm the milk (it should be very warm, but not hot; about 110°F on an instant-read thermometer). Gently stir in the yeast plus 1 tablespoon of the sugar. Set aside for 5 minutes.

2. In the bowl of a stand mixer fitted with the dough hook, combine the remaining sugar, the flour, butter, eggs, and salt. Mix on low for about 5 minutes, or until a shiny dough forms. If it's too wet, add up to 2 tablespoons additional flour.

3. Lightly flour the counter and briefly knead the dough by hand for 30 seconds.

4. Lightly oil a medium bowl and transfer the dough into it. Cover with a damp towel and place it in a warm corner of the kitchen to proof—90°F is ideal. Let the dough rise for 1½ to 2 hours, until it doubles in size.

5. To make the filling: In a small bowl, stir to combine the sugar, butter, and cinnamon. Set aside so the butter remains soft, but not soupy.

6. Lightly grease a 9-by-13-inch baking dish with butter or nonstick spray and line it with parchment paper.

7. Lightly punch down the dough in the bowl. Sprinkle flour on the counter, and roll out the dough to a 15-by-20-inch rectangle or until it's about ¼ inch thick.

8. Spread the filling evenly onto the dough with a flexible spatula.

9. Working carefully, roll the dough lengthwise into a log. Gently pull on both ends so it's even in height from end to end.

10. With a sharp knife, cut the dough into 2-inch slices and place them, cut-side up, in the prepared baking dish. Leave room in between for the rolls to double in size.

11. Cover with a damp towel, place in a warm corner, and let rise for another 30 minutes.

12. Preheat the oven to 375°F and place a rack in the middle.

13. To make the wash: In a small bowl, mix together the egg, milk, and vanilla. With a pastry brush, lightly dab the tops of the risen rolls with the egg wash.

14. Bake for 12 to 15 minutes, or until light golden brown (the internal temperature of the rolls will be 190°F).

15. Cool for 5 minutes in the pan, then frost with Cream Cheese Drizzle before serving. These are best when served immediately but can be reheated in a microwave.

MORE STICKY BUNS

There are endless ways to fill a sticky bun. Here are some of my favorite options—I encourage you to experiment with your own. In each case, combine the ingredients while waiting for the first rise, then spread it evenly on the dough before rolling.

CHOCOLATE FILLING

Dark brown sugar 1 cup, packed

Bittersweet chocolate pieces ¾ cup

Unsalted butter, soft 4 ounces (1 stick)

Ground cinnamon 1 teaspoon

CHAI FILLING

Dark brown sugar 1 cup, packed

Crystallized ginger, minced ½ cup

Unsalted butter, soft 4 ounces (1 stick)

Ground ginger 1 tablespoon

Ground cinnamon 2 teaspoons

Ground cardamom 2 teaspoons

Anise seeds, ground 1 teaspoon

Ground cloves ½ teaspoon

Freshly ground black pepper ¼ teaspoon

Sea salt ¼ teaspoon

BANANA GINGER

Dark brown sugar 1 cup, loose

Bittersweet chocolate pieces ¾ cup

Bananas, chopped 1 cup

Unsalted butter, soft 4 ounces (1 stick)

Honey 1 tablespoon

Ground ginger 1 tablespoon

Nutmeg, freshly ground 2 teaspoons

SAVORY FILLING

Parrano or Fontina cheese, shredded 1 cup

Unsalted butter, soft 3 ounces (¾ stick)

Olive oil 2 tablespoons

Fresh sage, minced 2 tablespoons

Fresh thyme, chopped 1 tablespoon

Sea salt 2 teaspoons

CAKES

Cakes are a special addition to any brunch, but are especially appropriate if the brunch is in honor of an occasion—a birthday, anniversary, or bridal shower. Cakes made for brunch can also be dessert at any other meal, or served at any other time of day. But don't expect these goodies to last very long once sliced and served.

USE A SCALE to measure the flour, and be sure to sift it before measuring.

USE SUPERFINE SUGAR when mixing cakes—the grain is smaller than regular granulated sugar, which makes it better suited to achieving a fine texture in a cake.

SCRAPE THE BOWL of your stand mixer after the eggs are added and again after all of the ingredients are added. Be sure to get all the way down to the bottom of the bowl, where a lot of ingredients tend to hide.

USE A CAKE TURNTABLE to assemble cakes—they make life much easier. The heavy, cast-iron variety is an investment but will last forever.

IN GENERAL, AVOID NONSTICK cake pans. Use plenty of oil-and-starch nonstick spray (Baker's Joy® is my preferred brand) and aluminum pans instead.

CINNAMON-SUGAR COFFEE CAKE

FOR THE TOPPING

Walnuts, chopped	½ cup
Dark brown sugar	¼ cup, packed
Superfine sugar	18 ounces (2¼ cups)
Unsalted butter, very cold	6 ounces (1½ sticks)
Ground cinnamon	½ teaspoon
Ground ginger	½ teaspoon, plus ¼ teaspoon
Kosher salt	½ teaspoon

FOR THE CAKE

Unbleached all-purpose flour	12 ounces (2½ cups)
Baking soda	¼ teaspoon
Milk	1 cup
Fresh lemon juice	¼ cup
Heavy cream	1 tablespoon
Vanilla extract	1 teaspoon
Sliced almonds or chopped walnuts	1½ ounces (⅓ cup)
Candied ginger, minced	2 tablespoons
Eggs	3
Egg yolks	3
Cinnamon-Sugar Glaze (page 51)	1 batch

This lightly spiced coffee cake is simply delicious and serves up plenty of temptation. Prepare the spiced sugar topping first and refrigerate it so the butter is very cold when dropped into the pan. To prevent the cake from sticking, use plenty of nonstick spray and invert the pan to remove the cake within minutes after removing it from the oven.

1. Preheat the oven to 325°F and place a rack in the middle. Thoroughly coat one 12-cup or two 4½-cup Bundt pans with nonstick cooking spray. Set aside.

2. To make the topping: In a small bowl, mix together the walnuts, brown sugar, 3 tablespoons of the superfine sugar, 2 tablespoons of the butter, the cinnamon, ½ teaspoon of the ginger, and ¼ teaspoon salt. Place the topping in the fridge.

3. In a large bowl, combine the flour, baking soda, remaining salt, and remaining ginger, and set aside. In another bowl, stir together the milk, lemon juice, cream, and vanilla and set aside.

4. In the bowl of a stand mixer fitted with the paddle attachment, mix the remaining butter, the remaining superfine sugar, the almonds and candied ginger on low speed for 3 to 4 minutes. Add the eggs and yolks one at a time. Stop and scrape down the sides of the bowl.

5. With the mixer on low, alternately add the dry and liquid ingredients in 3 batches. Stop the mixer, scrape the sides of the bowl, and run for 20 seconds on low speed to fully combine.

6. Remove the spiced sugar topping mix from the fridge and sprinkle it evenly into the prepared Bundt pan(s).

7. Scoop enough batter to fill the pans about three-quarters full.

8. Bake the larger cake for 45 to 50 minutes, or until it is golden brown and a wooden skewer inserted in the center comes out clean. Reduce the baking time to 30 to 35 minutes if using smaller pans.

9. Remove the cake from the oven and cool in the pan on a wire rack for 5 minutes. Invert the pan to slide the cake(s) onto the rack.

10. Once the cake has cooled completely, use a fork to drizzle it heavily with Cinnamon-Sugar Glaze. Store under a cake dome to retain moisture.

Cakes with a high sugar content baked in nonstick pans tend to develop tough surfaces. In nonstick pans, the batter bonds with itself, making a smooth and glassy surface instead of adhering just a little to the pan and making one that's crusty and crunchy. (My one exception to this is my Lemon Cranberry Bundt Cake.)

PIÑA-ORANGE-BANANA POUND CAKE

I love this combination of fruits as a beverage, so I wanted to bring it together as a dessert option for brunch. There's less fat in this batter than usual, so the banana flavor isn't covered up and the pineapple chunks stay suspended, but it also yields a crumb that's not quite as soft as the other cakes. If you're feeling adventurous, slice this for French toast!

1. Preheat the oven to 325°F and place a rack in the middle. Thoroughly coat a 12-cup Bundt pan with nonstick cooking spray. Set aside.

2. In a large bowl, mix together the flours, pineapple, potato starch, zest, salt, baking soda, and nutmeg and set aside. In a separate bowl, combine the bananas, orange segments, milk, sour cream, rum (if using), and vanilla. Set aside.

3. In the bowl of a stand mixer fitted with the paddle attachment, mix the butter and superfine sugar on low speed for 3 to 4 minutes. Add the eggs and yolks one at a time. Stop and scrape down the sides of the bowl.

4. With the mixer on low, alternately add the dry and liquid ingredients in 3 batches. Stop the mixer, scrape the sides of the bowl, and run for 20 seconds on low speed to fully combine.

5. Lightly sprinkle the prepared pan with turbinado sugar if desired. Scoop the batter into the pan to fill it about three-quarters full.

6. Bake for 45 to 50 minutes, or until the cake is golden brown and a wooden skewer inserted in the center comes out clean.

Unbleached all-purpose flour	12 ounces (2½ cups)
Whole-wheat flour	2 tablespoons
Dried pineapple, roughly chopped	½ cup
Potato starch	1 tablespoon
Orange zest	2 teaspoons
Kosher salt	½ teaspoon
Baking soda	¼ teaspoon
Nutmeg, freshly grated	¼ teaspoon
Bananas, mashed	2
Navel orange, segmented	1
Milk	¾ cup
Sour cream	2 ounces (¼ cup)
Dark rum	1 tablespoon (optional)
Vanilla extract	2 teaspoons
Unsalted butter, soft	4 ounces (1 stick)
Superfine sugar	12 ounces (1½ cups)
Eggs	3
Egg yolks	2
Turbinado sugar	for the pan (optional)
Orange Glaze (page 51)	1 batch

7. Remove from the oven and cool in the pan on a wire rack for 5 minutes. Invert the pan to slide the cake onto the rack.

8. Once the cake has completely cooled, use a fork to drizzle it heavily with Orange Glaze. Store under a cake dome to retain moisture.

LEMON-CRANBERRY BUNDT

This is a delicious Bundt cake with simple and classic flavors. I baked it to celebrate my first Father's Day while visiting my parents with my wife and daughter. It was a real treat to be able to bake something the whole family enjoyed. Because I was limited to what my parents had on hand, I used Arrowhead Mills unbleached white flour, and I think it contributed to the cake's light texture. I'm sure it could be reproduced with other brands, though. Always use fresh lemons, especially for the glaze. It makes a huge difference.

Unbleached all-purpose flour	12 ounces (2½ cups)
Cranberries, dried	4 ounces (½ cup)
Maple sugar or turbinado sugar	1 tablespoon
Sea salt	½ teaspoon
Baking soda	¼ teaspoon
Milk	¾ cup
Sour cream	4 ounces (½ cup)
Lemon, segmented	1
Maple syrup	1 tablespoon
Vanilla extract	½ teaspoon
Superfine sugar	20 ounces (2½ cups), plus extra for the pan
Unsalted butter, soft	6 ounces (1½ sticks)
Lemon zest	1 tablespoon
Eggs	4
Egg yolks	2
Lemon Glaze (page 51)	1 batch

1. Preheat the oven to 325°F and place a rack in the middle. Thoroughly coat a 12-cup nonstick Bundt pan with nonstick cooking spray. Set aside.

2. In a large bowl, mix together the flour, cranberries, maple sugar, salt, and baking soda and set aside. In a separate bowl, combine the milk, sour cream, lemon segments, maple syrup, and vanilla. Set aside.

3. In the bowl of a stand mixer fitted with the paddle attachment, mix the superfine sugar, butter, and zest on low speed for 3 to 4 minutes (see Note). Add the eggs and yolks one at a time. Stop and scrape the sides of the bowl.

4. With the mixer on low, alternately add the dry and liquid ingredients in 3 batches. Stop the mixer, scrape the sides of the bowl, and run for 20 seconds on low speed to fully combine.

5. Lightly sprinkle the prepared pan with superfine sugar if desired. Scoop the batter into the pan to fill it about three-quarters full.

6. Bake for 45 to 50 minutes, or until the cake is golden brown and a wooden skewer inserted in the center comes out clean.

Citrus Zest

7. Remove from the oven and cool in the pan on a wire rack for 5 minutes. Invert the pan to slide the cake onto the rack.

8. Once the cake has completely cooled, use a fork to drizzle it heavily with Lemon Glaze. Store under a cake dome to retain moisture.

NOTE: The batter won't get fluffy due to the ratio of sugar to butter and the fact that the oil in the lemon zest will break down the sugar and interfere with its ability to capture air. That's okay—we're accounting for that.

A nonstick pan and lots of nonstick pan spray is essential for this cake. Dried cranberries seriously stick to a conventional pan and no amount of glaze will fix the unsightly mess. It helps to chop the cranberries in half to make them lighter in the batter so they'll be distributed more evenly throughout the cake rather than fall to the bottom. But you can skip the chopping and just cream the butter, sugar, and lemon zest with the cranberries—the paddle will do most of the work for you.

BLUEBERRY BUNDT CAKE

This one is easy and delicious. Don't pass it up! The amount of cream and milk really makes for a moist crumb. Stir in the berries after the batter is in the Bundt pan if you want to keep some of the berries mixed throughout the cake. Otherwise just fold them in after the final mix.

Unbleached all-purpose flour	12½ ounces (2½ cups)
Potato starch	1 tablespoon
Sea salt	½ teaspoon
Baking soda	¼ teaspoon
Milk	⅔ cup
Heavy cream	⅔ cup
Vanilla extract	2 teaspoons
Superfine sugar	20 ounces (2¾ cups)
Unsalted butter	7 ounces (1¾ sticks)
Eggs	5
Fresh blueberries	1⅓ cups

1. Preheat the oven to 325°F and place a rack in the middle.

2. In a large bowl, mix together the flour, potato starch, salt, and baking soda and set aside. In a separate bowl, combine the milk, cream, and vanilla. Set aside.

3. In the bowl of a stand mixer fitted with the paddle attachment, mix the superfine sugar and butter.

4. Add the eggs one at a time. Stop and scrape the sides of the bowl.

5. With the mixer on low, alternately add the dry and liquid ingredients in 3 batches. Stop the mixer, scrape the sides of the bowl, and run for 20 seconds on low speed to fully combine.

6. Thoroughly coat a 12-cup Bundt pan with nonstick spray. Scoop the batter into the pan; it will nearly come to the top. Using a spatula, fold the blueberries into the batter.

7. Bake for 50 to 60 minutes, or until the cake is golden brown and a wooden skewer inserted in the center comes out clean.

8. Remove from the oven and cool in the pan on a wire rack for 5 minutes. Invert the cake onto the rack. Serve immediately. Store under a cake dome to retain moisture.

LEMON POUND CAKE

Unbleached all-purpose flour	11 ounces (2 cups plus 2 tablespoons)
Potato starch	1 tablespoon
Sea salt	½ teaspoon
Baking soda	¼ teaspoon
Milk	⅓ cup
Heavy cream	⅔ cup
Sour cream	2 ounces (¼ cup)
Lemons, segmented	2
Vanilla extract	1 teaspoon
Rum	2 tablespoons
Brandy	2 tablespoons
Boyajin lemon oil	½ teaspoon
Superfine sugar	18 ounces (2¼ cups)
Unsalted butter	6 ounces (1½ sticks)
Lemon zest	½, plus extra as needed
Eggs	5
Lemon Glaze (page 51)	1 batch

I baked this especially for Wally Amos for his seventy-fifth birthday. A friend of his asked me to make a lemon pound cake, his favorite, and I was happy to start building flavors and textures from scratch. Instead of my normal routine, I approached it from a new angle. I changed the "wet" ingredients to add a lot of cream and milk. The result: a cake that's nothing short of absolutely tender, moist, and delicate.

1. Preheat the oven to 325°F and place a rack in the middle.

2. In a large bowl, mix together the flour, potato starch, salt, and baking soda and set aside. In a separate bowl, combine the milk, cream, sour cream, lemon segments, vanilla, rum, brandy, and lemon oil. Set aside.

3. In the bowl of a stand mixer fitted with the paddle attachment, mix the superfine sugar, butter, and zest on low speed for 3 to 4 minutes.

4. Add the eggs one at a time. Stop and scrape the sides of the bowl.

5. With the mixer on low, alternately add the dry and liquid ingredients in 3 batches. Stop the mixer, scrape the sides of the bowl, and run for 20 seconds on low speed to fully combine.

6. Thoroughly coat a 12-cup Bundt pan with nonstick cooking spray. Set aside. Scoop the batter into the pan; it will nearly come to the top.

7. Bake for 45 to 50 minutes, or until the cake is golden brown and a wooden skewer inserted in the center comes out clean.

8. Remove from the oven and cool in the pan on a wire rack for 5 minutes. Invert the pan to slide the cake onto the rack.

9. Once the cake has completely cooled, drizzle it heavily with Lemon Glaze. Sprinkle with additional lemon zest, if desired. Store under a cake dome to retain moisture.

AMARETTO BUTTER CAKES

Unbleached all-purpose flour	6 ounces (1¼ cups), sifted
Baking soda	⅛ teaspoon
Kosher salt	⅛ teaspoon
Cayenne pepper	⅛ teaspoon
Ground cinnamon	1 pinch
Sour cream	4 ounces (½ cup)
Amaretto	2 tablespoons
Brandy	1 teaspoon
Vanilla extract	½ teaspoon
Superfine sugar	9 ounces (1 cup plus 2 tablespoons), plus extra for the pans
Unsalted butter, soft	3 ounces (¾ stick)
Sliced almonds, roasted	1 ounce (½ cup)
Eggs	2
Egg yolks	1
Confectioners' sugar	for sprinkling (optional)
Cinnamon-Sugar Glaze (page 51)	1 batch (optional)

Mini cakes are a delight for any time of day, and they make a great option for dessert after a hearty meal like brunch. Guests can take them to go or just sneak off to have one when the rest of the party is staggering around looking for a seat to recline and complain about how full they feel. Don't hesitate to try it with the cayenne—pepper blends very well with sweets. By adding just a pinch, the cayenne will stay in the background to enhance the taste, similar to the way a pinch of salt enhances other flavors without overwhelming them.

1. Preheat the oven to 325°F and place a rack in the middle. Thoroughly coat fifteen 2-ounce brioche pans with non-stick cooking spray.

2. In a medium bowl, combine the flour, baking soda, salt, cayenne, and cinnamon and set aside. In a separate bowl, combine the sour cream, amaretto, brandy, and vanilla. Set aside.

3. In the bowl of a stand mixer fitted with the paddle attachment, mix the sugar, butter, and almonds on low speed for 3 to 4 minutes.

4. Add the eggs and yolks one at a time. Stop and scrape the sides of the bowl. Alternately add the dry and liquid ingredients in 3 batches.

5. Lightly sprinkle the pans with superfine sugar.

6. Scoop ¼ cup batter into each pan. Bake for approximately 15 minutes, or until the cakes are golden brown and a toothpick poked into the center of one comes out clean.

7. Remove the cakes and let them cool on a wire rack for no more than 2 minutes. Invert each pan to release the cakes onto the rack. Don't wait until the pan cools entirely or the cakes will get stuck.

8. Serve naked or, once the cakes have cooled completely, dust with confectioners' sugar or drizzle heavily with Cinnamon-Sugar Glaze.

NOTE: You can also make one 9-cup Bundt cake with this recipe. Bake at 325°F for 45 to 50 minutes.

COCONUT CAKE WITH MERINGUE BUTTERCREAM

Pastry flour	10 ounces (2⅓ cups), sifted
Baking powder	1 teaspoon
Sea salt	½ teaspoon
Baking soda	¼ teaspoon
Coconut milk	1 cup
Coconut oil (see Note), melted	2 tablespoons
Vanilla extract	1 teaspoon
Superfine sugar	12 ounces (1½ cups)
Unsalted butter, soft	4 ounces (1 stick)
Eggs	3
Yolks	2
Cooked Meringue Icing (recipe follows)	1 to 2 batches
Shredded, sweetened coconut	2 (6 ounce) packages

An elaborate layer cake isn't always on order for brunch, but it makes a great centerpiece and a fantastic way to end the meal. There's also nothing wrong with having it around for seconds throughout the day. For the photograph, I doubled the recipe to make four cake pans, which gave me a really tall cake.

1. Preheat the oven to 325°F and place a rack in the middle. Line two 8-by-2-inch or 7-by-2-inch cake pans with parchment paper and set aside.

2. In a medium bowl, mix together the flour, baking powder, salt, and baking soda and set aside. In a separate bowl, combine the coconut milk, oil, and vanilla. Set aside.

3. In the bowl of a stand mixer fitted with the paddle attachment, mix the sugar and butter on low speed for 3 to 4 minutes.

4. Add the eggs and yolks one at a time. Stop and scrape the sides of the bowl.

5. Alternately add the dry and liquid ingredients in 3 batches. Stop the mixer, scrape the sides of the bowl, and run for 20 seconds on low speed to fully combine.

6. Bake for approximately 25 minutes, or until the cakes are golden brown across the top and a toothpick inserted into the center comes out clean.

7. Remove from oven, let them cool in the pans for 5 minutes, and then invert each pan to release the cakes onto a wire rack.

8. To assemble the layer cake, slice each cake horizontally in half once with a serrated knife. Spread the icing between each layer, using about ½ cup per layer. Mound and swirl the meringue on the top and sides. Sprinkle on the coconut as desired.

NOTE: Vegetable oil can be substituted for the coconut oil, but the soft and somewhat subtle layers of coconut flavor will be sacrificed.

COOKED MERINGUE ICING

This is light, bright, and airy—and it's fat free! Depending on the number of layers in your cake, and how much icing you like to use, you may want to double this recipe. I recommend you do that in two batches, though; otherwise the meringue might overflow the mixing bowl.

Egg whites	5
Superfine sugar	12 ounces (1½ cups)

1. In the bowl of a stand mixer fitted with the whisk attachment, whip the egg whites on high speed into a meringue with a stiff peak.

2. In a small, heavy-bottomed saucepan, bring 1 cup of the sugar and ¼ cup water to 250°F on a candy thermometer.

3. Just before the syrup reaches 250°F, turn the mixer on high and sprinkle the remaining sugar into the meringue.

4. Slowly pour the melted syrup into the meringue while the mixer is on high speed. Continue to whip until the meringue is very stiff and the heat is distributed throughout the bowl. Allow the meringue to cool before frosting the cake.

SAVORY

These are the dishes that really make breakfast a meal—and brunch memorable. Potatoes in all forms (but mostly fried) are expected, but don't lose sight of the flavor that vegetables bring to the plate.

BREAKFAST MEATS

Meat and fish take their place at the breakfast table in many countries around the world. Breakfast buffets in hotels across Europe will always offer an array of cold meats, while the Scandinavian countries set out a smorgasbord of meats, cheeses, and smoked fishes. Here in the States, our choice of bacon and sausages probably reflects our British heritage, given that those meats feature prominently in the traditional English breakfast as well.

THE DOS AND DON'TS OF BACON GREASE

Don't pour bacon fat down the drain. That includes washing globs of it off of baking sheets or frying skillets. This will clog your pipes and the sewer system. Don't add it to your compost either, as any kind of meat scraps or grease will attract vermin.

Instead, wipe it out of the pan with paper towels, wrap them in a plastic bag and toss it in the trash. Better yet, bottle and refrigerate it for use in future cooking.

POTATOES

Nowadays I can get potatoes in almost any color, from white to yellow to red to purple, and I like to use a variety of spuds in my recipes. Yukon Gold and Red Bliss are good all-purpose potatoes for frying; they're more waxy than Russets and hold their shape well. Wash potatoes thoroughly to remove all the starch. Chefs generally fill a bucket and run cold water over the cut spuds, sometimes for hours. At home a tall serving pitcher should work well enough. Once it's full of water, reduce the flow to a trickle to save water and slosh the taters around every few minutes. Dry the potatoes in a salad spinner and let them drip-dry for up to 10 minutes.

VEGGIES AND SALADS

Too often we get caught in the thinking that breakfast or brunch should be "sinful" to be good. That's just not the case. Vegetables served at their peak add color and flavor that's beyond compare. Making the most of seasonal fruits and vegetables is much easier to do now that farmer's markets featuring local produce are easier to come by. Take whatever is in season and do as little as possible to it. Focus on the raw flavors of the earth and share them with those you love.

TIPS FOR SUCCESSFUL POTATOES

- Cut the potatoes in uniform pieces. Frying is a quick-cooking method and you want all the pieces to be cooked through.

- When frying, use a mono- or polyunsaturated oil with a high smoking point, like refined canola, grapeseed, or rice bran oil.

BANGERS AND MASH

Yellow or red new potatoes	4
Unsalted butter	2 ounces (½ stick)
Salt	1 tablespoon
Milk	½ cup or more
Vegetable oil	2 tablespoons
Sausages	2 to 4 links (about 1 pound)
Yellow or other sweet onion	1

In my early days of living in DC, one of my best friends would make a plate of bangers and mash on Sunday mornings. Dominic was over from London for about a year, working in radio journalism. The dish was new to me, and I always marveled at the meticulous preparation he put into the meal. This classic British dish of sausages served over mashed potatoes with onions and gravy is a delight on the fork and a treat to have as brunch or supper on a cold winter day. Try to find authentic "bangers," which are fat English or Irish breakfast sausages.

1. Preheat the oven to 350°F and set the rack on the middle shelf.

2. Bring a pot of water to a rolling boil. Add the potatoes and cook until tender, about 10 to 15 minutes.

3. Rinse the potatoes under cold water and peel them, then place them in a large bowl. Using a fork, mash them with the butter and salt or return them to the pot and use an electric hand mixer. Add in the milk as needed to make them smooth and creamy. Cover and set aside.

4. Heat the oil in a medium skillet over medium heat and gently cook the sausages, turning frequently.

5. Meanwhile, slice the onion and set it aside. Remove the sausages and cook the onion in the fat left in the pan until tender.

6. Arrange the potatoes on an ovenproof platter. Place the bangers and onions on top and bake for 20 minutes.

SUGAR- AND SALT-CURED SALMON

Lox and bagels, bagels and lox—cured salmon is a staple breakfast food in many cultures. Curing salmon is a process of chemically "cooking" the fish. The salt and sugar create a hostile environment for bacteria while drawing a lot of fluid from the fish. This removes the threat of food-borne illness and yields a wonderfully soft texture and unmatched flavor.

I was introduced to the process by a friend who cured fish for cocktail parties. When I tasted his home-cured salmon, I was stunned and instantly inspired. It was so soft. It melted in my mouth. There were distinct flavors from spices, citrus, and sugars that he used. It tasted nothing like store-bought cured salmon—not that they're all that bad. This was just so much better. The following weekend, my wife, Pam, and I visited our local market, bought a whole salmon fillet, and cured it. It was the start of a real adventure.

To get the full flavor of the cured fish, serve it with thinly sliced breads—either toasted bagels or pumpernickel toast points. Use only the freshest salmon fillets purchased from a reliable fishmonger.

TRADITIONAL CURED SALMON

Makes 2 pounds

Salmon fillet **2 pounds**

Vodka **2 tablespoons**

Sugar **1¼ cups**

Kosher salt **¾ cup**

Freshly ground black pepper **2 teaspoons**

Caraway seeds **2 teaspoons**

Fresh dill **½ bunch, stems removed (about 4 to 6 cups)**

Lemon, **thinly sliced 1**

1. Cut the fillet into 2 even portions. Place them in a large bowl and sprinkle on the vodka.

2. Combine the sugar, salt, pepper, and caraway in a bowl and toss to combine. Add half of the mixture to the fillets and toss to completely coat the fish.

3. Lay down some parchment paper on the counter to make a work space. Place both fillets on the paper.

4. Cover one fillet with layers of the following: half of the dill leaves, half of the lemon slices, the rest of the sugar and salt mixture, the remaining dill and lemon slices. Place the other fillet on top.

5. Tightly wrap the whole sandwich of ingredients in plastic wrap. I always double wrap it and apply a lot of pressure to make a super-tight seal.

6. Place the wrapped fish in casserole dish and weight it down: Place a smaller casserole dish on top filled with a few heavy jars or canned goods. You want 4 to 5 pounds of pressure on top of the fish.

7. Refrigerate for 24 hours. Remove the top weight, plastic wrap, dill, and lemon slices. A lot of liquid will drip from the fish. Shake off any liquid and wrap it again in fresh plastic wrap. Cover with the same weights and refrigerate for another 24 hours.

8. Remove the plastic wrap and shake off any of the curing agents. *Do not* rinse.

9. With a very sharp, long, thin knife, slice the fish as thinly as possible. Serve on its own next to a plate of eggs, with toast points, or in a salad.

10. Store any leftovers tightly wrapped in the fridge. They will keep for up to 1 week.

HOT AND SPICY CURED SALMON

Going spicy is not the traditional path for curing fish, but cayenne and orange zest do marry well with salmon fillets. Two different salts are called for to bring in as much variety of flavor as possible. Sea salts are great because no two are the same in taste and structure. Kosher salt, while not as complex in flavor as sea salt, offers a great structure and good taste without the bite of regular table salt.

Makes 2 pounds

Salmon fillet **2 pounds**

Vodka **3 tablespoons**

Granulated sugar ½ **cup**

Sugar ¾ **cup**

Sea salt ¼ **cup**

Kosher salt ½ **cup**

Cayenne pepper ½ **teaspoon**

Orange zest **2 tablespoons**

Fresh dill ½ **bunch, stems removed (about 4 to 6 cups)**

Fresh rosemary **4 to 5 sprigs**

Prepare as you would Traditional Cured Salmon (page 172).

DIPPING SAUCES FOR CURED FISH

These easy dipping sauces pair well with either of the salmon cures. Serve in a separate bowl, along with toast points or bagel chips.

INSTANT COCKTAIL SAUCE

Makes 1 cup

Mayonnaise ½ **cup**

Chili sauce ½ **cup**

Worcestershire sauce ¾ **teaspoon**

Freshly ground black pepper ½ **teaspoon**

Liquid smoke ¼ **teaspoon**

Salt ¼ **teaspoon**

Combine all the ingredients in a bowl, stir to blend, and serve. Cover and refrigerate any leftovers.

EASY TARTAR SAUCE

Makes ¾ cup

Hard-boiled egg **1**

Mayonnaise ½ **cup**

Diced pickles or relish **2 tablespoons**

Fresh lemon juice **2 teaspoons**

Worcestershire sauce **1 teaspoon**

Capers **1 teaspoon**

Dijon mustard **1 teaspoon (optional)**

Freshly ground black pepper ½ **teaspoon**

Salt ¼ **teaspoon**

Fresh chives, chopped **1 teaspoon**

In a small bowl, mash the egg and then stir in the remaining ingredients, folding in the chives last. Cover and refrigerate any leftovers.

SOY DIPPING SAUCE

Powerful flavor components that command respect, fish sauce and shrimp paste can be found in an Asian grocery or international foods aisle at your local grocery store.

Makes 1 cup

> Mayonnaise ¾ **cup**
>
> Soy sauce **2 tablespoons**
>
> Sriracha hot sauce **2 tablespoons**
>
> Fresh ginger, peeled and grated **1 tablespoon**
>
> Scallions, sliced **1 tablespoon**
>
> Rice vinegar **2 teaspoons**
>
> Fresh chives, chopped **1 teaspoon**
>
> Dried shrimp paste ½ **teaspoon**
>
> Fish sauce ¼ **teaspoon**

Combine all the ingredients in a bowl, stir to blend, and serve. Cover and refrigerate any leftovers.

SKILLET-FRIED HASH BROWNS

Hash browns are just one way to add a special touch to brunch or breakfast any day of the week. Don't wait for a special occasion—start frying! Everyone loves potatoes in a skillet, no matter what's going on.

Yukon Gold or Russet potatoes	4 (2 pounds)
Vegetable oil	½ to ¾ cup
Kosher salt	as needed

1. Preheat the oven to 275°F and place a rack in the middle.

2. Scrub the potatoes but do not peel them. Grate the potatoes and rinse them well with cold water 3 times. Spin dry in a salad spinner and let them drip-dry for at least 5 minutes.

3. Heat ¼ cup of the oil in a large skillet over medium to high heat. Be generous—if they stick to the pan, they'll fall apart.

4. Sprinkle about 2 teaspoons of the salt in the pan, drop in enough potatoes to cover the surface, and then press firmly to flatten with a metal spatula. Add more salt to taste and cook for about 4 minutes.

5. When the potatoes are browned well at the edges, use the spatula to cut the potatoes into quarter sections to flip more easily.

6. Flip and continue to pan fry for another 3 to 4 minutes. The potatoes should have ragged edges that are browned and crisp.

7. Keep the hash browns warmed in the oven. Repeat with the remaining potatoes. Add oil and salt as necessary.

To control the splatter, I use a wire mesh splatter guard for skillet frying and a pot with high sides for deep frying. Either way, I always have the windows open and the vent cranked all the way!

HEIRLOOM TOMATO SALAD

Vine-ripened heirloom tomatoes	3 large
Olive oil	1 tablespoon (or less)
Sea salt or kosher salt	to taste
Fresh basil leaves	6 to 8

One of the best ways to serve delicious, ripe fruits and vegetables is with barely anything added. Accents that let the flavors of the food itself shine are the sign of a well-made dish.

1. Wash and slice the tomatoes.

2. Arrange them on a plate, drizzle with the oil, and sprinkle with salt. Slice the basil into thin ribbons, or leave whole, if desired, and drape it on top of the tomatoes.

HOME FRIES

Yukon Gold potatoes	2 large (1 pound)
Red new potatoes	2 large (1 pound)
Blue potatoes	2 large (1 pound)
Vegetable oil	3 cups, or more as needed
Sea salt	to taste
Spices of choice (such as paprika, garlic and onion powder, black pepper)	to taste

I fry these potatoes twice to yield a crisp exterior. If you don't have the time, just fry them once in oil at about 350°F for 7 to 10 minutes. They won't be crispy fries, but they sure are good.

Your guests will dive into fried potatoes any way you dish them up. I get bonus points from the family when I add a few blue potatoes to the mix. The color and flavor variations are nice, so try a few new types with your next meal.

1. Scrub, peel (if you'd like—it's okay to leave the skin on), and cut the potatoes into uniform pieces; ½- to ¼-inch matchsticks or cubes work well.

2. Immediately place the cut potatoes into a bowl and run cold water over them until they are submerged. Continue running the water in a thin stream for about 10 minutes. Occasionally, twirl the potatoes to release more starch.

3. Drain off the water and spin the potatoes well in a salad spinner to dry. Allow them to drip-dry for 5 to 10 minutes.

4. Meanwhile, heat the oil in a heavy-gauge stockpot to 350°F on a deep-fry thermometer.

5. Carefully drop the potatoes into the frying oil. I prefer using a ladle or tongs. Fry the potatoes undisturbed for 5 minutes. Remove and set them aside on a baking sheet lined with paper towels or brown paper bags laid flat. Chill them in the fridge for at least 1 hour or up to 4 hours.

6. Preheat the oven to 275°F and place a rack in the middle. Reheat the oil to 375°F. Fry the potatoes for about 4 minutes, or until they're a nice golden brown. Remove one to test for doneness. Careful—it will be hot!

7. Remove the remainder with tongs and place them on a baking sheet lined with paper towels or brown paper bags laid flat. Sprinkle with salt and any spices you wish and put the fries in the warmed oven until you're ready to serve.

MUSHROOM BREAD PUDDING

Savory bread puddings are a great alternative to the sweet variations and make a fantastic comfort dish all year round.

1. Preheat the oven to 350°F and place a rack in the middle. Grease a 1-quart baking dish and sprinkle it with salt.

2. Dice the seeded zucchini into ¼-inch pieces.

3. Add the butter and 2 pinches salt to a medium skillet over medium heat. Add the mushrooms and zucchini and sauté for 3 minutes, or until soft.

4. In a large bowl, combine the vegetables with the bread, milk, Fontina, stock, ricotta, and egg. Toss well. In a small bowl, mix together the nutmeg, paprika, mace, and salt and pepper to taste.

5. Spread the bread mixture into the prepared baking pan, and lightly sprinkle the spice mixture over the top.

6. Bake for 35 minutes, or until nicely browned. Cool at least 15 minutes before cutting and serving. Reheat individual servings in microwave or with a steamer.

Sea salt	as needed
Zucchini, seeded	1 medium
Unsalted butter	2 tablespoons
Fresh mushrooms (cremini, button, portobello, shiitake), sliced	2 cups
Bread (of your choice), torn into small cubes	3 cups
Milk	3 to 4 cups
Fontina, shredded	1 cup
Chicken or vegetable stock	½ cup
Ricotta	¼ cup
Egg	1
Nutmeg, freshly grated	½ teaspoon
Paprika	½ teaspoon
Ground mace	¼ teaspoon
Freshly ground black pepper	to taste

GRILLED MUSHROOM SALAD WITH CHÈVRE

Fresh portobello mushrooms	3 caps
Fresh cremini mushrooms	8 ounces
Fresh shiitake mushrooms	8 ounces
Olive oil	¼ cup
Balsamic vinegar	2 tablespoons
Soy sauce	1 tablespoon
Fresh sage, minced	1 tablespoon
Kosher salt	1 teaspoon
Chèvre	2 tablespoons
Fresh chives, chopped	1 teaspoon

Grilled vegetables have a ton of flavor, and mushrooms are especially appetizing because they absorb so much of the marinades and the smokiness of the grill itself. If you prefer, place the mushroom mixture on a baking sheet lined with parchment paper and roast in a 375°F oven for 25 to 40 minutes.

My wife and I spend a lot of time in Kennet Square, Pennsylvania, a wonderful small town that's also the mushroom capital of the United States! I draw a lot of inspiration from the annual mushroom festival held there every September.

1. Gently remove the stems from the portobellos and use a butter knife or spoon to remove the gills. Lightly rinse the portobellos, creminis, and shiitakes, and pat them dry before setting aside to air dry.

2. Slice the portobello caps into ¼-inch-wide strips. In a medium bowl, toss together the mushrooms, oil, vinegar, soy sauce, sage, and salt. Marinate for 30 minutes to 3 hours.

3. Soak five bamboo skewers in water for at least 30 minutes to prevent them from burning.

4. Start a hot fire (about 450°F to 500°F) on one side of the grill about 30 minutes before you want to begin grilling. Scrape the grate clean so it'll be ready for use.

5. Skewer the cremini mushrooms. Place the skewers and remaining 'shrooms directly on the grate away from the heat.

6. Cook with indirect heat for 7 to 10 minutes, depending on the heat of the fire, until the 'shrooms are crisped a bit. Use a metal spatula to lift the items off the grill. Turn if desired, but cooking on one side should be sufficient.

7. Let them cool to room temperature. Loosely arrange the mushroom mixture on a serving plate and crumble the chèvre on top. Garnish with freshly chopped chives.

BACON HOME FRIES

These are delicious. How could they not be? They're briefly fried in bacon fat and butter. It's not the end of the world if we have a little fun and set aside worries about health risks for one side dish at a meal. If this sounds like a lot of hot air, then skip to the Oven-Roasted Taters (page 186)! For everyone else, enjoy!

Yukon Gold potatoes	6 (3 pounds)
Smoked bacon	3 strips
Canola oil	½ cup
Salt	to taste

Always ask for bacon that is cured without nitrates. Bacon is not health food, but you are certainly better off without the artificial nitrates.

1. Preheat the oven to 350°F and place a rack in the middle.

2. Scrub, peel, and dice the potatoes into ¼- to ⅛-inch cubes. Place the potatoes in a bowl or serving pitcher and run them under a thin steady stream of cold water for 10 minutes to wash off the starch. Spin in a salad spinner and let them drip-dry for at least 5 minutes.

3. Put the bacon in a cold, tall-sided, cast-iron skillet and cook slowly over medium heat for 10 minutes, until it is crisp. (Starting with a cold pan keeps the strips long and prevents curling.)

4. Remove the bacon and set aside. Add the oil to the bacon fat and add slices of potatoes to cover the bottom of the pan. Do not let them overlap.

5. Cook the slices undisturbed. Turn once after 3 to 4 minutes. Cook for another 3 minutes, then transfer the potatoes to a baking sheet lined with paper towels or brown paper bags laid flat. Put them in the oven.

6. Cook the next batch and repeat until all of the slices are pan fried. Hold the potatoes in the oven for no longer than 30 minutes before serving.

7. Lightly sprinkle with salt before serving.

APPLE, BEET & CARROT SALAD

This simple but delicious combination of flavors gets a touch of beauty from the beets, which lend delicate color to everything they touch. Gently cook the beets and carrots separately until al dente, then combine them and hold in the fridge to let the beets work their magic on the carrots and apples.

Fresh beets	3 to 4 medium
Fresh carrots	1 pound
Fresh Golden Delicious apples	2
Fresh mint	3 to 4 leaves
Sea salt	to taste
Sugar	to taste

1. Set two medium-size pots over medium-high heat and bring 1½ quarts of water, as well as 1 teaspoon of salt, to a boil in each. Add the beets (do not peel) to one pot and boil until tender, about 20 minutes. Dunk in an ice bath to stop the cooking.

2. While the beets are cooking, peel the carrots and slice on the bias (diagonal) so they are ¼ inch thick. Add them to the second pot and boil until tender, about 6 minutes. Dunk in an ice bath to stop the cooking.

3. Cut the cooked beets into slices a little less than ¼ inch thick.

4. Core and slice the apples a little less than ¼ inch thick, leaving the skin on if you like.

5. Slice the mint into thin ribbons.

6. Combine the beets, carrots, apples, and mint in a large bowl and toss with a rubber spatula. Add salt and sugar to taste. Since this salad tastes best served cold, hold in the fridge, covered, until you're ready to serve.

OVEN-ROASTED TATERS

Red new potatoes, medium	5 (2½ pounds)
Sweet potato, peeled	1 (½ pound)
Bacon	3 strips, cut into pieces
Olive oil	2 tablespoons
Unsalted butter, melted	2 tablespoons
Fresh rosemary, minced	1 tablespoon
Kosher or sea salt	2 teaspoons

Each tiny cube is like a micro burst of 'tater heaven, generously slathered and sprinkled with the simple flavors of butter, olive oil, and sea salt. Roast with care until the potatoes are soft and tender, but firm to bite. And don't resist adding the sweet potato—it's not just great for color, but adds great depth of flavor as well.

1. Preheat the oven to 375°F and place a rack in the middle. Line a baking sheet with parchment paper or a silicone baking mat.

2. Scrub the red potatoes (do not peel) and cut them into ⅛-inch dice. Place the potatoes in a bowl or serving pitcher and run them under a thin, steady stream of cold water for 10 minutes to wash off the starch.

3. Cut the sweet potatoes into ⅛-inch dice, place them in a separate bowl, and run them under a thin, steady stream of cold water for 10 minutes to wash off the starch.

4. Spin dry all the potatoes in a salad spinner and let them drip-dry for at least 5 minutes.

5. In a large bowl, toss together the potatoes, bacon, oil, butter, rosemary, and salt.

6. Spread the mixture onto the prepared baking sheet and roast for 45 to 50 minutes, or until tender all the way through.

When I need small pieces of raw bacon to add flavor, I like to cut it with kitchen shears. Slicing raw bacon with a knife is difficult because the fatty meat slides off the cutting board, and a lot of equipment must be washed thoroughly to avoid cross-contamination. Shears save time and hassle.

ROASTED CAULIFLOWER SALAD

I discovered cauliflower very late in life, but once I did, I became a huge fan. It's easy and fast, and it tastes delicious on its own or paired with other goodies—especially when roasted. I like the idea of monochromatic dishes that are set off by one or two accents; in this case, I've used almonds and lemon zest.

Cauliflower	1 head
Olive oil	¼ cup
Sea salt	1 tablespoon
Blanched almonds	½ cup
Lemon juice	2 tablespoons
Garlic	1 head
White balsamic vinegar	3 tablespoons
Golden raisins	½ cup
Lemon zest	from 2 lemons

1. Preheat the oven to 375°F and place a rack in the middle.

2. Cut the stem out of the cauliflower and separate the florets. Combine the florets with the olive oil and salt in a large bowl and toss with a flexible spatula.

3. Spread the cauliflower on a parchment-lined baking sheet, setting the bowl aside to be used again—do not rinse it. Roast the cauliflower for 20 to 25 minutes or until the stalks of florets become slightly translucent.

4. Toss the almonds and lemon juice in the same bowl. Add a little olive oil and a dash of salt if there wasn't much left. Spread the almonds in an even layer on another parchment-lined baking sheet and roast for 5 to 7 minutes.

GRILLED CHICKEN SALAD

I prefer to grill chicken over any other cooking method, especially if I'm using the meat for chicken salad. The fire, smoke, and dry heat add great flavor. Since I don't glop on tons of mayonnaise, the flavor of the grill and the additional ingredients really come through. Placing the meat next to, but not above, the heat source is a great way to grill. The hot, dry air, as opposed to the flames, cooks the meat well and locks in the juices. Don't place the meat above the heat—flare-ups will char the chicken to a crisp or dry it out too much. With a gas grill, crank the burner to high; for charcoal or wood, start the fire on one side of grill and add fuel to keep the blaze hot.

1. Start the grill, focusing the heat to one side.

2. Rinse and dry the chicken. Using kitchen shears or a sharp knife, cut out the backbone. Toss the chicken with the salt, oil, and vinegar. Push on the breastbone until the chicken flattens.

3. When the grill is very hot, place the chicken skin-side up on the grate next to the heat. Keep it at least 2 to 3 inches away from the heat. Close the lid and cook, without turning, for approximately 30 minutes or until the white meat reaches 165°F.

4. Remove and cool on a cutting board or roasting pan.

5. To make the chicken salad, combine all the ingredients except the salt and pepper in a large mixing bowl and toss well with a rubber spatula.

6. Pull the meat from the grilled chicken using your fingers, or cut it away from the bone and chop into small pieces.

7. Add the chicken to the other ingredients and toss to combine. Season with salt and pepper to taste. Chill before serving.

FOR THE GRILLED CHICKEN	
Whole chicken	3 to 4 pounds
Kosher or sea salt	1½ tablespoons
Olive oil	2 tablespoons
Balsamic vinegar	2 tablespoons

FOR THE SALAD	
Celery, diced	3 stalks
Gala apples, peeled and diced	2
Cucumber, peeled and sliced	½
Nayonnaise or mayonnaise	2 tablespoons
Plain Greek yogurt	½ cup
Smoked Gouda, cubed	½ cup
Scallions	3
Grainy mustard	2 tablespoons
Liquid smoke	½ teaspoon
Balsamic vinegar	1 tablespoon
Salt	to taste
Freshly ground black pepper	to taste

GRILLED ROMAINE

Romaine lettuce	1 head
Olive oil	¼ cup
Balsamic vinegar	2 tablespoons
Salt	to taste
Freshly ground black pepper	to taste

There is no better way to impress your buds—and taste buds—than with a new way of presenting the same old dish. Grilled salad is easy to prepare and looks delicious enough even for kids to want to eat their vegetables! I especially like grilling romaine because it tames the bitterness in the stem, but the head is sturdy enough to withstand the heat of the fire. I like to slice each grilled half lengthwise and serve one-quarter with freshly cracked black pepper as a side. It might seem like a lot of lettuce, but the presentation is dramatic.

1. Start a fire and distribute the coals on one side of the grill. Bring the temperature to about 350°F.

2. Cut the lettuce in half lengthwise, beginning at the stem, but do not separate the leaves.

3. Thoroughly rinse out any dirt and shake to dry.

4. Drizzle the oil and vinegar onto the flat sides of the romaine and sprinkle with salt and pepper.

5. Place the flat sides directly on the grates over a medium flame. Cook for about 5 minutes, or until the top leaves are charred and the stem is well seared.

6. Tear off any leaves that are too charred to serve. Slice lengthwise to divide the lettuce into sections for serving.

ASPARAGUS WITH BUTTER

Unsalted butter	3 tablespoons
Kosher or sea salt	½ teaspoon
Asparagus	½ pound

My favorite way to prepare these simple-yet-elegant garden spears is to sauté them lightly in butter and salt, then serve warm.

1. Melt the butter in a medium-size skillet over medium heat.

2. Add the salt, distributing it evenly across the pan.

3. Add the asparagus and gently roll the spears in the pan to coat them with the butter and salt.

4. Cook until the asparagus turns bright green and barely begins to go limp. If necessary, add 1 to 2 tablespoons of water and cover briefly to speed up the cooking.

5. Remove the asparagus to a serving dish and serve immediately.

HOMEMADE CROUTONS

Homemade croutons are easy to make and add a lot of personality to your presentation. Way back when I was in college, a good friend of mine had a pig roast at his family's farm, and his dad made homemade croutons. They were the talk of the party—and for good reason . . . I still remember them! Surprise your friends and family with a simple delight that makes a lasting impression.

Use your favorite one- or two-day-old bread, but don't let it go rock-hard stale. Roasting the bread locks in flavor while slowly drying it out and toasting it, so you need some moisture in there.

Bread, torn or diced	3 cups
Olive oil	¼ cup
Unsalted butter	3 tablespoons
Garlic cloves, pressed	2
Balsamic vinegar	3 tablespoons
Sea salt	1 teaspoons
Black pepper	½ teaspoon
Onion powder	1 teaspoon
Paprika	½ teaspoon
Thyme	1 teaspoon

1. Combine all of the ingredients in a large bowl and toss with a flexible spatula to coat.

2. Spread the croutons in an even layer in a disposable aluminum pan and place on the grill grates, but not directly over the flame.

3. Cook for approximately 10 to 15 minutes. Turn occasionally or as needed. Alternately, roast on a parchment paper–lined baking sheet in a preheated 375°F oven for 10 to 15 minutes.

RESOURCES

Here is some helpful information about baking at high altitudes or in high humidity, converting measurements into metric quantities, and the importance of weighing certain ingredients.

HIGH-ALTITUDE ADVISORY

I find the difference between sea-level and high-altitude recipes interesting. When I'm baking at high altitude (5,000 feet above sea level), these are the basics I review before I crack the first egg.

THE TIMING IS WACKY. You know what they say about dry heat. Because there's less water vapor in the air to trap and retain the heat, it doesn't feel as hot. At higher altitudes, there is less water vapor, too. There's also much less of the other naturally occurring atmospheric gases—like oxygen—in the air. Without the same quantities of gases to trap and retain the heat as there are at sea level, the air doesn't conduct the oven's heat as effectively. The result is that it takes longer for cakes to bake.

THE BATTER MIGHT MISBEHAVE. Thinner air also means less pressure on the cake batter as it bakes. Cakes will rise faster with less effort. And rapidly rising batter is vulnerable to collapsing unless we help out by giving the structure a slight boost.

THE QUANTITIES ARE DIFFERENT. To help the batter behave better, reduce the baking soda or baking powder and bump up the amount of protein from flour or eggs to make it all work.

BAKING IN HIGH HUMIDITY

Humidity, atmospheric pressure, and temperature always have an effect on baking. Sometimes it's very noticeable; other times, it isn't. In the nation's capital, it's the humidity that I combat the most. The chocolate butter cakes tend to sink in the center right around mid-May—that's when high humidity and rising summer temperatures become a regular part of our weather report. To adjust, I increase the temperature by a few degrees and bake for a few minutes longer. This effectively burns off the excess moisture in the air that otherwise weighs the cake down and slows the baking.

CONVERSION CHARTS

WEIGHT EQUIVALENTS The metric weights given in this chart are not exact equivalents, but have been rounded up or down slightly to make measuring easier.

AVOIRDUPOIS	METRIC
¼ oz	7 g
½ oz	15 g
1 oz	30 g
2 oz	60 g
3 oz	90 g
4 oz	115 g
5 oz	150 g
6 oz	175 g
7 oz	200 g
8 oz (½ lb)	225 g
9 oz	250 g
10 oz	300 g
11 oz	325 g
12 oz	350 g
13 oz	375 g
14 oz	400 g
15 oz	425 g
16 oz (1 lb)	450 g
1½ lb	750 g
2 lb	900 g
2¼ lb	1 kg
3 lb	1.4 kg
4 lb	1.8 kg

VOLUME EQUIVALENTS These are not exact equivalents for American cups and spoons, but have been rounded up or down slightly to make measuring easier.

AMERICAN	METRIC	IMPERIAL
¼ tsp	1.2 ml	
½ tsp	2.5 ml	
1 tsp	5.0 ml	
½ Tbsp (1.5 tsp)	7.5 ml	
1 Tbsp (3 tsp)	15 ml	
¼ cup (4 Tbsp)	60 ml	2 fl oz
cup (5 Tbsp)	75 ml	2.5 fl oz
½ cup (8 Tbsp)	125 ml	4 fl oz
cup (10 Tbsp)	150 ml	5 fl oz
¾ cup (12 Tbsp)	175 ml	6 fl oz
1 cup (16 Tbsp)	250 ml	8 fl oz
1¼ cups	300 ml	10 fl oz (½ pint)
1½ cups	350 ml	12 fl oz
2 cups (1 pint)	500 ml	16 fl oz
2½ cups	625 ml	20 fl oz (1 pint)
1 quart	1 liter	32 fl oz

OVEN MARK	F	C	GAS
Very cool	250–275	130–140	½–1
Cool	300	150	2
Warm	325	170	3
Moderate	350	180	4
Moderately hot	375–400	190–200	5–6
Hot	425–450	220–230	7–8
Very hot	475	250	9

WEIGHT EQUIVALENTS

ALL-PURPOSE FLOUR It's critical to weigh certain ingredients for successful baking. Dry ingredients—especially flour—compress easily into a cup measure, making the scoop-and-level method inaccurate. The most accurate way to measure flour is to weigh it after sifting. Here are the weight equivalents for common volume measurements of all-purpose flour.

WEIGHT	VOLUME
1 ounce	3 tablespoons
2 ounces	¼ cup + 2 tablespoons
3 ounces	½ cup + 1 tablespoon
4 ounces	¾ cup + ½ teaspoon
5 ounces	1 cup
6 ounces	1 cup + 1 tablespoon
7 ounces	1¼ cups + 2 tablespoons
8 ounces	1½ cups + 1 tablespoon
9 ounces	1¾ cups + ½ teaspoon
10 ounces	2 cups
11 ounces	2 cups + 1 tablespoon
12 ounces	2¼ cups + 2 tablespoons
12½ ounces	2½ cups
13 ounces	2½ cups + 1 tablespoon
13½ ounces	2½ cups + 3 tablespoons
14 ounces	2¾ cups + ½ teaspoon
14½ ounces	2¾ cups + 1 tablespoon +1 teaspoon
15 ounces	3 cups

SUPERFINE GRANULATED SUGAR Superfine granulated sugar, the sugar generally used in this book, weighs about 8 ounces per cup. (Standard table sugar, or typical granulated sugar, weighs 7 ounces per cup. It has a larger crystal than extra-fine granulated, so less mass fits into a one-cup measure.)

WEIGHT	VOLUME
1 ounce	2 tablespoons
2 ounces	¼ cup
3 ounces	6 tablespoons
4 ounces	½ cup
5 ounces	½ cup + 2 tablespoons
6 ounces	¾ cup
7 ounces	¾ cup + 2 tablespoons
8 ounces	1 cup
12 ounces	1½ cups
16 ounces	2 cups
20 ounces	2½ cups
24 ounces	3 cups

OTHER INGREDIENTS

INGREDIENT	WEIGHT	VOLUME
butter	4 ounces	8 tablespoons (1 stick)
confectioners' sugar	4¼ ounces	1 cup

INDEX

Note: Page references in *italic* refer to illustrations.

ACKNOWLEDGMENTS

My wife, Pam, is the most patient, loving, and gracious person I know. She deserves not only *my* thanks, but thanks from anyone who finds this book enjoyable, because she made a lot of sacrifices so that I could write it. This project came with all of the usual challenges that come with gathering great ideas and putting them on paper, but the process involved many extra challenges as well, because it was written and photographed during our daughter's first year, a time that included a lot of errands, drives to Kennet, and time apart. Thank you, Pam, for your support, which made it possible for me to focus on my work.

Thanks to my mom, Beatrice, who showed me a world that inspired my curiosity. Nothing could be a greater gift.

Thanks to my dad, Leon, who recently passed. Dad, your work taught me to understand how ingredients can relate to one another.

Thanks to my sisters, Lenora and Liz, and to the many other loving members of my family who were there for me over the years, encouraging me to follow my dreams.

Thank you, Mary Cairns, for opening up your home to my wife and our family as we adjusted to parenthood, and for allowing me to test recipes in your kitchen.

Thanks to Kate, Emma, Christine, Art and the other taste testers at Chatham Financial—it's always fun.

Thanks to the countless customers at CakeLove and Love Café who have tasted and given me feedback on my creations over the years, and specifically on the creations in this book.

A heartfelt thanks to the baristas, cooks, bakers, customer sales representatives, cake decorators, dishwashers, drivers, and cupcake frosters at Love Café and CakeLove. Your commitment to excellence and friendly, informed service for our customers helps make my dream come true every day.

Thanks to Neil Barret and Julia Cohen for opening their beautiful home, which makes a splendid backdrop for the photos!

Thanks to Lisa Cherkasky for her wonderful food styling and very helpful hints throughout the photo shoot; to Joshua Cogan for capturing the light and showing the world what the words on the page say; to Mary Meyers for her organizational talents and sourcing prowess; and to Kim Lamore for her tireless work on set and enthusiastic stewardship of CakeLove.

Thanks to my editor, Jennifer Levesque, for shepherding this book through the editing process, especially when I could not, and to Alissa Faden for another wonderful design.

ABOUT THE AUTHOR

Warren Brown is the founder and owner of CakeLove and Love Café. His organization includes multiple retail storefronts in the Washington, DC, and Baltimore areas (see www.cakelove.com for more information). He is a former host of *Sugar Rush* on the Food Network and author of *CakeLove: How to Bake Cakes from Scratch* and *United Cakes of America: Recipes Celebrating Every State*, both published by Stewart, Tabori & Chang.

Brown graduated with a B.A. in history from Brown University and with a law degree and a master's in public health from George Washington University. He worked in public health and then practiced health care law in the office of the Inspector General for the U.S. Department of Health and Human Services until 2000, when he left to pursue his passion for cooking. He found his calling in baking and opened his first bakery, CakeLove in Washington, DC, in 2002.

Since then, Brown has been recognized not only for his baked goods but also for his entrepreneurial spirit. He has been featured in numerous national media, including television (*The Oprah Winfrey Show*, the *TODAY* show, *Dateline*, *Fox News Sunday*), publications (*GQ*, *INC Magazine*'s 26 Entrepreneurs We Love, *People*, *Reader's Digest*, *Southern Living*, *Black Enterprise*, *The American Lawyer*, *Kiplinger's*, *Personal Finance*, the *Washington Post*, the *Washington Times*, *Washingtonian*), and advertising campaigns for American Express and Dell.

He lives in Washington, DC, with his wife and daughter.